Photography: John Lee Studio
Roy Rich, Angel Studio
Christian Delu

© Copyright 1975 Purnell & Sons Ltd.
Published 1976 by Sampson Low, Berkshire House,
Queen Street, Maidenhead, Berkshire.
Printed in Italy by Poligrafici Calderara
SBN 562 000267

Four Seasons Cookery Books

Summer

Audrey Ellis

Drawings by Marilyn Day

Sampson Low

Contents

Useful information

Metric measures: The new standard measure holds 3 dl. (300 ml.) which is just under ½ pint.

1. Sets of metric spoons are available now in the following capacities:— 15 ml. (1 tablespoon), 10 ml., 5 ml. (1 teaspoon), 2.5 ml. The full set comprises two additional spoons, 20 ml. and 1.25 ml. but these are optional. To avoid confusion with earlier (Imperial) standard equipment and existing domestic cutlery, the term 'cup' will be replaced by 'measure' and spoons will eventually be referred to by capacity rather than tablespoon and teaspoon.

2. The new metric measuring jugs contain 1 litre, or ½ litre. The litre jug is marked at 7.5 dl., ½ litre/5 dl., 1.5 dl. and 1 dl.

3. The metric unit of weight is the kilogram (kg.) which is 1000 g. or 2.2 lb. Where recipes give ingredients in ounces, the metric unit of 25 g. has been found practical. Spring balance scales marked in metric or dual-marked in metric and Imperial are available. The pointer shows 1 kilo/2¼ lbs. and indicates divisions of 500 g./18 oz., 250 g./9 oz. and 125 g./4½ oz. Smaller units are marked at intervals of 25 g. Most food packs show weights in both systems, e.g. 4 oz. (113 g.) or 500 g. (1 lb. 1½ oz.).

Oven temperature chart

	°F	°C	Gas Mark
Very cool	225	110	¼
	250	130	½
Cool	275	140	1
	300	150	2
Moderate	325	170	3
	350	180	4
Moderately hot	375	190	5
	400	200	6
Hot	425	220	7
	450	230	8
Very hot	475	240	9

Checking quantities: As personal tastes in seasoning vary, quantities of salt and pepper are left to individual choice unless critical to the success of the recipe. All spoon measures are level. All recipes are to serve 4 unless otherwise indicated.

Seasonal cooking: Many of the recipes given in this book can be used in other seasons. For example there is a summer season for avocados and a winter season. Some items are constantly available frozen or canned.

Acknowledgments

The author and publishers thank the following for their help in supplying photographs for this book:
The Pasta Information Centre, p. 26.
Summer Avocados, p. 29, p. 65.
Californian Wine Institute, p. 30, p. 39.
Tabasco Pepper Sauce, p. 33, p. 34
Papino Pawpaws, p. 35.
The U.S. Rice Council, p. 36, p. 40, p. 42.
Taunton Cider Company Limited, p. 37.
Buxted Brand products by Ross Poultry Limited, p. 38.
John West Foods, p. 44.
The British Sausage Bureau, p. 44, p. 48.
New Zealand Lamb Information Bureau, p. 46.
Carmel Avocado Information Bureau, p. 49.
The Mushroom Information Bureau, p. 50.
The Tupperware Company, p. 52.
The National Dairy Council, p. 53, p. 65.
The Swiss Cheese Union, Inc., p. 55.
Ambrosia Creamed Rice, p. 69.
British Sugar Bureau, p. 72.

Introduction

Welcome those lazy, hazy days of summer with carefree catering plans which make the most of seasonal fresh fruits, vegetables and salads, now in glorious abundance. Eating out of doors is a pleasure we all look forward to each year, and if leafy June is followed by flaming July, take full advantage by eating 'en plein air' as often as possible; whether it is a picnic far afield or a back garden barbecue. Many recipes for both are given in this volume, some really unusual, so if you've never sampled savoury fresh herb scones with assorted cold meats, or barbecued honey fruit kebabs, here is your opportunity.

The buying guide for the season is bound to put the spotlight on fruit; most of us jam, preserve, bottle or freeze some of these summer delights but nothing beats the fresh fruit itself, warm and fragrant from picking. Choosing perfect berry fruits is one of the few remaining tests of the skilled housewife and shopper. On a summer Saturday you will find in every country town market, urban high street or shopping parade, a choice of strawberries ranging in quality from fair to first rate at prices which vary mysteriously without any apparent rhyme or reason. It is an art to select those which represent the best value, or to be brave enough to decide that a family outing cum picnic should take the form of a strawberry-picking spree at a farm. A few preserves you will never see in the shops are still worth making however busy you are at this time of year; what about Pickled cherries, or Spiced grape butter?

As an extra aid to making up menus from the seasonal meal section, every dish is marked as being simple for everyday use, or sophisticated for entertaining, by the star system shown below. Sometimes this means that the dish take less time to prepare rather than being inexpensive; but even the most spectacular recipes are not costly.

The Summer months are busy ones for freezer owners with all that tempting fruit to pack whole, sliced, puréed or made into sauces and freezer jams. My section on home freezing carries this a step further; there are sorbets, ice creams and mousses to make which ensure Summer-fresh sweets in midwinter as well. Good advice on freezing fish and poultry and gardening hints are given in this, the busiest season of all for those who grow for their own freezers. The barbecue party plan completes my Summer selection, which will, I am confident, help you to spend less time in the kitchen and yet enjoy delicious food and fun out of doors in the sunshine.

Sophisticated

Simple

Audrey Ellis

Buying guide for the season

Soft berry fruits: Any housewife who has bought a punnet of such fruit at what she imagines to be a bargain price, and discovered that it was full of small, unripe or mouldy berries under a thin layer of choice fruit, knows how hard it is to pick out the best. Under-ripe fruit is recognisable by its pale colour or may even be white on the side that has not been exposed to the sun. It is not sufficiently sweet or juicy, and has not developed full flavour. If picked in wet weather, moulds develop very quickly, often within 24 hours; so be extra careful when buying shortly after a rainy period. Over-ripe fruit may smell delicious but has a suspiciously strong perfume. It becomes discoloured, brownish and mushy rapidly, although it is not a dead loss because the better parts of the fruit can be utilised in a purée. Only experience teaches the exact shade of colour which denotes perfect ripeness in any particular variety.

Imported strawberries usually ripen en route and are often of a long pointed shape not grown here. Home-grown berries are fully ripened on the plant and sweetest in flavour; Royal Sovereign and Cambridge Vigour (slightly more conical in shape) being the most popular varieties. Both are light scarlet when ripe. Two other popular large berries are Red Gauntlet, and Grandee, both rounder in shape and deep crimson when fully ripe. The green leafy hull should always be moist and fresh—if wrinkled and greyish the fruit has been a long time on its way to the shop. Raspberries are usually sold hulled because the hull has a tendency to be left behind when the fruit is ripe enough to pick from the cane. The summer crop available in July and August produces the largest berries which should be a rich, slightly pinkish red, but in most years a second crop or a late-fruiting variety of smaller berries comes on in September. Loganberries which are larger and longer than raspberries, have a distinctive flavour and are very sour if eaten before fully ripe; they must be deep purple in colour. Gooseberries are excellent for cooking, mostly oval in shape and bright green ripening to yellowish green or a dusky red. The dessert varieties, of which Howard's Leveller is the most popular, is rounder, larger, almost hairless and ripens to a very rich golden yellow. Most culinary varieties are downy, or quite hairy, but this property disappears in cooking. Currants are not often to be seen in the shops these days. Blackcurrants are most often available, the best having large black berries, since even dark red ones are under-ripe. They are sold ready stripped from the stalk. Red and white currants are sold on the stalk and some loss of weight must be expected in stripping. Very few reach the shops, and as each currant is so tiny, they are really only suitable to use as a decoration or to make currant jelly.

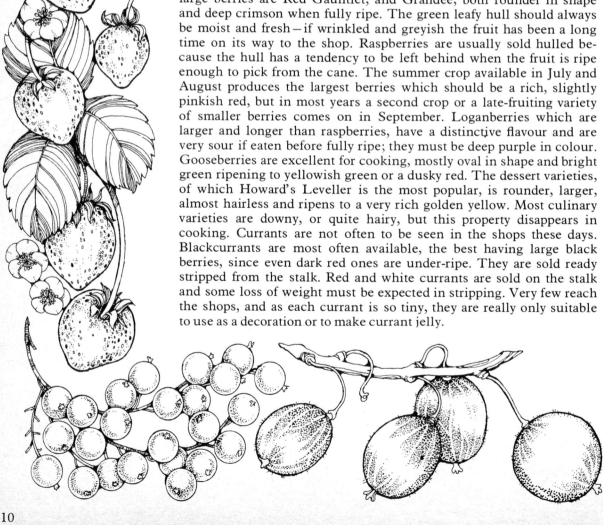

The soft fruit season falls mainly within the months of June, July and August, with a few second crops and late varieties to be hoped for in September.

Melons: These fruits are difficult to judge for ripeness. Some have a distinct perfumed smell close to the stalk scar, some will yield slightly to discreet pressure at this point and others deepen to a warmer shade of colour when fully ripe. The honeydew melon is available most of the year and according to the country of origin may have a deeply corrugated green skin or a much smoother yellow or greenish white skin. All have the easily recognisable oval shape and the flesh may be pale green or yellow. The two most delicately flavoured melons are the Charentais and the Ogen and of these the former is Summer's queen—yellowy green skin with greenish stripes and a deep pinkish orange flesh with an exquisite perfumed flavour. The other most richly flavoured melon is the cantaloupe, also with a yellowy green skin and indented green stripes ripening to golden yellow and with perfumed juicy orange flesh. Watermelons have a definite season from about May to September and are the only ones to have a pink flesh and black seeds. Unripe melons can be ripened by placing unwrapped anywhere consistently warm, even the airing cupboard.

Shellfish

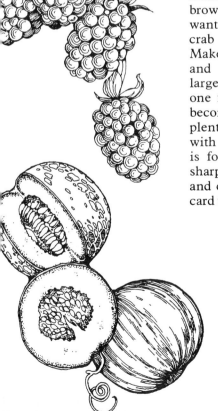

Although we are used to buying molluscs (those with hinged shells like mussels, oysters and scallops) in their original homes, it is only rarely that we have the opportunity to shop for crustaceans in the shell, particularly crabs and lobsters, although prawns and their smaller brethren shrimps are often bought this way. Crabs, which are brownish grey when alive, turn dull red when cooked. Few people want to cope with a live crab. As the business of dressing the cooked crab is a nuisance, many fishmongers sell undressed ones cheaply. Make sure the crab has both claws attached as these are full of meat and are often sold separately by the fishmonger. The males have larger claws, but the females have the delicious red 'coral'. A good one feels heavy for its size. Lobsters, dark blueish grey when alive, become light scarlet when cooked. The male has larger claws and plenty of claw meat but the female tends to be larger in the body with more tender flesh, and again the succulent coral which, in fact, is formed by the eggs. If the lobster is fresh, the tail springs back sharply when straightened. Mussels—these you really must buy live and cook yourself. If the shells do not close when sharply tapped discard them as the mussel is dead and unfit to eat.

Summer – early

Fish	Meat, Poultry and Game	Vegetables	Fruit
Bass	Duck	Asparagus	Apples
Bream	English lamb	Aubergines	Apricots
Brill	Guinea fowl	Avocados	Bilberries
Cockles	Pigeon	(summer)	Blackcurrants
Cod	Quail	Beetroot	Cherries
Coley	Rabbit	Broad beans	Figs
Conger eels	Turkey	Broccoli	Gooseberries
Crab	Venison	Cabbages	Grapefruit
Crawfish		Cauliflowers	Grapes
Dabs		Celery	Lemons
Dover soles		Chicory	Limes
Eels		Courgettes	Loganberries
Grey mullet		Cucumbers	Mangoes
Haddock		French beans	Melons
Hake		Garlic	Oranges
Herring		Globe artichokes	Peaches
Lemon sole		Lettuces	Pears
Lobster		Mange tout peas	Pineapples
Mackerel		Mustard & cress	Plums
Mock halibut		New carrots	Raspberries
Plaice		Okra	Redcurrants
Prawns		Onions	Rhubarb
Rainbow trout		Parsley	Strawberries
Salmon		Pears	
Shrimps		Peppers	
Turbot		Potatoes	
Whitebait		Radishes	
Witch		Spinach	
		Spring onions	
		Tomatoes	
		Turnips (new)	
		Watercress	

Summer – late

Fish	Meat, Poultry and Game	Vegetables	Fruit
Bass	Duck	Aubergines	Apples
Bream	English lamb	Avocados (summer)	Apricots
Brill	Grouse	Beetroots	Blackberries
Cod	Guinea fowl	Broad beans	Blackcurrants
Coley	Hare	Cabbage	Cherries
Conger eels	Pigeon	Carrots	Damsons
Crab	Quail	Cauliflower	Figs
Dabs	Rabbit	Celery	Gooseberries
Dover soles	Snipe	Courgettes	Grapefruit
Dublin Bay prawns	Turkey	Cucumbers	Grapes
Eels	Venison	Fennel	Greengages
Haddock		French beans	Lemons
Hake		Globe artichokes	Loganberries
Halibut		Horseradish	Melons
Herring		Leeks	Mulberries
Lemon sole		Lettuces	Nectarines
Lobster		Onions	Oranges
Mackerel		Parsley	Peaches
Plaice		Parsnips	Pears
Portuguese oysters		Peas	Persimmons
Prawns		Peppers	Pineapples
Rainbow trout		Runner beans	Plums
Red mullet		Shallots	Raspberries
Salmon		Spinach	Redcurrants
Shrimps		Spring onions	Strawberries
Skate		Sweetcorn	Walnuts
Soles		Tomatoes	Watermelons
Turbot		Turnips	Whitecurrants
Whiting		Vegetable marrows	

Certain items such as mushrooms, bananas, chicken etc. are omitted as they are available from various sources through the year with little variation in price.

Midsummer — Pack-a-picnic time

When the weather is just too good to stay indoors and the children are on holiday from school, the weekend urge to picnic on a grassy bank may seize you at any time. Picnic food should be simple but not stodgy. Our menus are for a party of eight.

Filling fare for the family

Fresh herb scones

Imperial/Metric
4 oz./125 g. wholemeal flour
4 oz./125 g. plain flour
½ teaspoon bicarbonate of soda
1 teaspoon baking powder
½ teaspoon salt
2 oz./50 g. butter
½ teaspoon dried mixed herbs
2 heaped tablespoons chopped fresh herbs
¼ pint/1½ dl. natural yogurt

American
1 cup wholewheat flour
1 cup all purpose flour
½ teaspoon baking soda
1 teaspoon baking powder
½ teaspoon salt
¼ cup butter
½ teaspoon dried mixed herbs
2 tablespoons chopped fresh herbs
generous ½ cup plain yogurt

Mix together the flours, bicarbonate of soda, baking powder and salt and rub in the butter. Stir in the remaining ingredients and knead to form a soft dough. Roll out lightly and cut into 2 inch/5 cm. rounds. Place on greased baking trays and bake in a moderately hot oven (400°F, 200°C, Gas Mark 6) for 10-15 minutes, until golden brown. Serve split and buttered with slices of canned ox tongue, chopped ham and pork and party sausages. *Note:* Don't forget to take the can opener and a suitable knife.

Sausage and apple pielets

Imperial/Metric
1 lb./450 g. shortcrust pastry
1 medium cooking apple
1 small onion
1 lb./450 g. pork sausage meat
1 egg, beaten

American
1 lb. basic pie dough
1 medium baking apple
1 small onion
1 lb. bulk pork sausage
1 egg, beaten

Roll out the pastry and use to line eight deep bun tins. Re-roll trimmings and cut out eight 3-inch/7.5 cm. circles for lids. Grate the apple and onion and mix with the sausagemeat. Divide the filling between the pastry cases, mounding it up well in the centres. Brush the edges of the pastry with a little beaten egg, place on the lids and crimp edges together with finger and thumb to seal. Add a little water to the remaining egg and brush over the tops of the pielets. Bake in a moderately hot oven (400°F, 200°C, Gas Mark 6) for 30 minutes, or until golden brown. Cool on a wire rack.

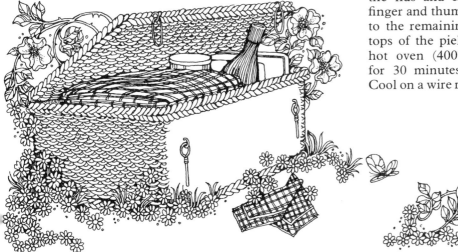

Filled celery sticks: Remove all the outer sticks from a head of celery, wash and 'string' them to remove coarse outer fibres. Beat together 8 oz./225 g./½ lb. curd cheese with 2 tablespoons chopped brown pickles and salt and pepper to taste. Press the mixture into the hollows of the sticks firmly and smooth the tops level. Cut into approximately 4 inch/10 cm. lengths and pack in pairs with a divider between the filled surfaces.

 # Frosty chocolate bananas

Imperial/Metric
8 oz./225 g. plain chocolate
4 bananas
8 oz./225 g. peanuts, chopped

American
½ lb. milk chocolate
4 bananas
1 cup chopped peanuts

Melt the chocolate in a basin over a saucepan of hot water. Cut each banana in half crosswise and insert a wooden pick into the end of each banana half. Transfer the melted chocolate to a shallow dish. Roll the banana halves in the chocolate, and then in the chopped peanuts. Place on a tray lined with greaseproof paper and freeze until firm. Wrap individually in plastic cling wrap and return to the freezer. Makes 8.
Note: These will not melt for an hour at least if packed in an insulated bag.

An elegant 'déjeuner sur l'herbe'

 # Individual smoked salmon quiches

Imperial/Metric
1 lb./450 g. shortcrust pastry
1 oz./25g. butter
2 medium onions, chopped
8 oz./225g. smoked salmon pieces
2 eggs
½ pint/3 dl. milk
salt and pepper

American
1 lb. basic pie dough
2 tablespoons butter
2 medium onions, chopped
½ lb. smoked salmon pieces
2 eggs
1¼ cups milk
salt and pepper

Roll out the pastry and use to line eight 4 inch/10 cm. shaped foil flan cases. Chill. Melt the butter and use to fry the onion gently until soft. Chop the smoked salmon roughly, mix with the onion and divide between the pastry cases. Beat together the eggs and milk with seasoning to taste and pour over the filling. Bake in a moderately hot oven (400°F, 200°C, Gas Mark 6) for 25-30 minutes.

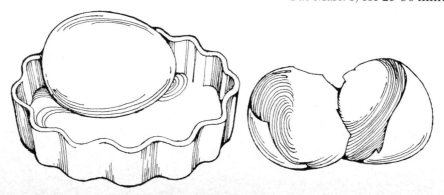

Avocado cream

Imperial/Metric
2 large avocados
6 tablespoons French
  dressing
2 tablespoons mayonnaise
2 tablespoons double
  cream
juice of ½ lemon
salt and pepper

American
2 large avocados
7 tablespoons Italian
  dressing
2 tablespoons mayonnaise
2 tablespoons heavy cream
juice of ½ lemon
salt and pepper

Peel the avocados, halve them, remove the stones and thinly slice the flesh. Place in a shallow dish with the dressing and allow to stand for 1 hour. Blend or mash until smooth and add the mayonnaise, lightly whipped cream and the lemon juice. Season to taste and beat well. Divide the mixture between 8 individual polythene containers, cover the surface with freezer film and seal them. Store in the refrigerator until ready to pack. Serve with spiced chicken drumsticks.

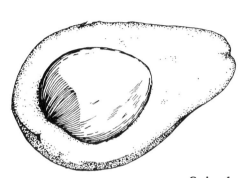

Spiced chicken drumsticks: Sprinkle 16 chicken drumsticks with a mixture of 2 tablespoons soy sauce, 1 tablespoon Worcestershire sauce and 1 teaspoon ground coriander. Cook under a hot grill, turning several times, and basting with the spicy mixture, for about 20 minutes, until cooked through. Cool and wrap in pairs in freezer film. Serve with Avocado cream.

Smothered peaches

Imperial/Metric
12 oz./350 g. sugar
1 teaspoon almond essence
8 large peaches
½ pint/3 dl. soured cream
6 oz./175 g. demerara sugar
3 oz./75 g. flaked almonds,
  toasted

American
1½ cups granulated sugar
1 teaspoon almond extract
8 large peaches
1¼ cups cultured sour cream
¾ cup light brown sugar
1 cup slivered almonds,
  toasted

Dissolve the white sugar in ¾ pint/4 dl./2 cups water, add the almond essence and simmer for 5 minutes. Pour boiling water over the peaches to loosen the skins and remove them. Add the peaches to the syrup and poach for 7-8 minutes, according to the ripeness of the fruit. Remove from the heat and allow to cool. Take out the peaches, halve and remove the stones. Slice the peach halves and divide between 8 small polythene containers. Reduce the remaining syrup to ¼ pint/1½ dl./generous ½ cup and spoon over the fruit. Beat the soured cream until smooth and spread a layer over each dessert. Mix together the demerara sugar and toasted almonds and sprinkle thickly over the soured cream. Seal and chill until ready to pack.

Salads to take with you

Pippin salad

Imperial/Metric
3 dessert apples
1 celery heart
1 small green pepper
few lettuce leaves
4 oz./125 g. cream cheese
16 walnut halves
paprika pepper
dressing:
¼ pint/1½ dl. double cream
1 teaspoon sugar
½ teaspoon salt
1 tablespoon tarragon
  vinegar or lemon juice
1 teaspoon French mustard
freshly ground black
  pepper

American
3 eating apples
1 celery heart
1 small green pepper
few lettuce leaves
½ cup cream cheese
16 walnut halves
paprika pepper
dressing:
generous ½ cup whipping
  cream
1 teaspoon sugar
½ teaspoon salt
1 tablespoon tarragon
  vinegar or lemon juice
1 teaspoon French mustard
freshly ground black
  pepper

First make the cream dressing. Mix together the cream, sugar and salt, then gradually add the vinegar or lemon juice, mustard and pepper to taste. Peel and core the apples and cut into small chunks. Chop the celery heart. Deseed and chop the pepper finely. Mix together the dressing, chopped apple, celery and pepper. Line a plastic bowl with lettuce leaves, and pile the apple mixture in the centre. Divide the cream cheese with a teaspoon into 8 small balls, press a walnut half into each side and use these to surround the salad. Sprinkle lightly with paprika pepper and cover.

Apple and blue cheese salad

Imperial/Metric
1 large lettuce
2 dessert apples
juice of 1 lemon
2 oz./50 g. Danish blue or
  Stilton cheese
4 tablespoons French
  dressing

American
1 large lettuce
2 eating apples
juice of 1 lemon
½ cup crumbled Stilton
  cheese
4 tablespoons Italian
  dressing

Wash the lettuce, pat the leaves dry with soft kitchen paper and tear up the larger leaves. Peel and core the apples and cut into slices across the fruit. Toss the slices lightly in the lemon juice to prevent discolouration. Crumble the cheese and mix with the dressing. Drain the apple slices and fold into the cheese mixture, then combine with the lettuce just before packing.

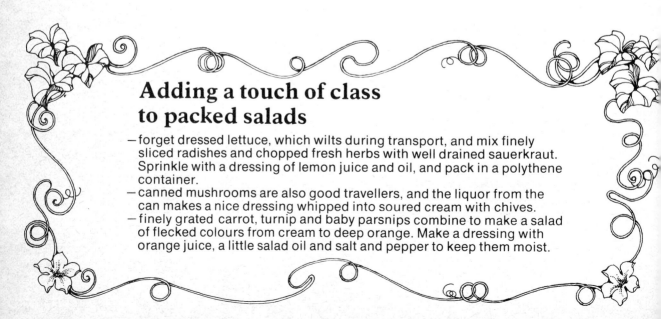

Adding a touch of class to packed salads

— forget dressed lettuce, which wilts during transport, and mix finely sliced radishes and chopped fresh herbs with well drained sauerkraut. Sprinkle with a dressing of lemon juice and oil, and pack in a polythene container.
— canned mushrooms are also good travellers, and the liquor from the can makes a nice dressing whipped into soured cream with chives.
— finely grated carrot, turnip and baby parsnips combine to make a salad of flecked colours from cream to deep orange. Make a dressing with orange juice, a little salad oil and salt and pepper to keep them moist.

Starters

Choose from a colourful selection of jewel-bright soups including one made with beetroot. Use fresh herbs while they are at their best now, just before harvesting, in small savoury tartlets, and try out more delectable shellfish starters from this group.

Fresh green pea soup

Imperial/Metric
2 chicken stock cubes
1 teaspoon sugar
juice of ½ lemon
1 large potato, sliced
1 large onion, sliced
1 large lettuce, shredded
1½ lb./700 g. green peas
salt and pepper
½ pint/3 dl. double cream

American
2 chicken bouillon cubes
1 teaspoon sugar
juice of ½ lemon
1 large potato, sliced
1 large onion, sliced
1 large lettuce, shredded
1½ lb. green peas
salt and pepper
1¼ cups whipping cream

Dissolve the stock cubes in 1 pint/generous ½ litre/2½ cups water, add the sugar, lemon juice, potato, onion, lettuce and peas. Bring to the boil, cover and simmer for 20 minutes. Sieve or liquidise the mixture and add a further 1 pint/generous ½ litre/2½ cups boiling water. Reheat and adjust seasoning. Stir in the cream and serve hot or cold. Serves 8.

Clear beetroot soup

Imperial/Metric
1 large raw beetroot
2½ pints/1½ litres beef stock
1 large carrot, grated
1 large onion, chopped
salt and pepper
1 teaspoon dried dill weed
    or 1 tablespoon chopped
    fresh dill

American
1 large raw beet
6 cups beef broth
1 large carrot, grated
1 large onion, chopped
salt and pepper
1 teaspoon dried dill weed
    or 1 tablespoon chopped
    fresh dill

Peel the beetroot, chop a little of it into neat dice and reserve for the garnish. Grate the remainder coarsely and place in a saucepan with the stock and other vegetables. Cover and simmer for 25-30 minutes, until all the vegetables are very tender. Taste and correct the seasoning. Strain, add the diced beetroot and cook for 8 minutes. Serve sprinkled with dill.

Courgette and potato soup

Imperial/Metric
8 oz./225 g. new potatoes
3 courgettes
1 large onion, chopped
1 oz./25 g. butter or
    margarine
1 pint/generous ½ litre
    chicken stock
1 bouquet garni
salt and pepper

American
½ lb. new potatoes
3 small zucchini
1 large onion, chopped
2 tablespoons butter or
    margarine
2½ cups chicken broth
1 bouquet garni
salt and pepper

Scrub the skins off the new potatoes and dice. Thinly slice the courgettes. Sauté the potatoes, courgettes, and onion in the butter for 5 minutes. Add the chicken stock and bouquet garni. Season with salt and pepper. Cover and simmer for 20 minutes until the vegetables are tender. Adjust seasoning, and remove bouquet garni.

Watercress soup

Imperial/Metric
1 stick celery
6 small white onions
1 clove garlic
2 tablespoons oil
1 teaspoon dried thyme
1 bay leaf
1 bunch watercress
1 tablespoon flour
2 chicken stock cubes
1½ pints/scant 1 litre
    boiling water

American
1 stalk celery
6 small white onions
1 clove garlic
2 tablespoons oil
1 teaspoon dried thyme
1 bay leaf
1 bunch watercress
1 tablespoon all purpose
    flour
2 chicken bouillon cubes
scant 4 cups water

Chop the celery and a little of the leaves, quarter the onions and crush the garlic. Cook the vegetables gently in the oil until limp but not coloured. Add the thyme and bay leaf. Chop the watercress roughly, add to the pan, sprinkle on the flour and stir well. Gradually add the stock cubes dissolved in the water and bring to the boil, stirring constantly. Simmer for 20 minutes and serve at once hot. Or, serve chilled, garnished with single cream.

Three bean soup

Imperial/Metric
8 oz./225 g. white haricot
  beans
8 oz./225 g. red kidney
  beans
8 oz./225 g. French beans
1 large onion
1 clove garlic
8 oz./225 g. tomatoes
1 small red sweet pepper
2 tablespoons oil
2 medium potatoes, diced
salt and pepper
2 tablespoons chopped
  basil

American
½ lb. white navy beans
½ lb. red kidney beans
½ lb. green beans
1 large onion
1 clove garlic
½ lb. tomatoes
1 small red sweet pepper
2 tablespoons oil
2 medium potatoes, diced
salt and pepper
2 tablespoons chopped
  basil

Soak the dried beans overnight in cold water, then drain. Trim and halve the French beans. Finely chop the onion, crush the garlic, peel and chop the tomatoes and deseed and chop the pepper. Heat the oil and use to fry the onion and garlic until softened. Reserve 2 tablespoons of chopped tomato and add the remainder to the pan with the beans, potato and water to cover. Season and bring to the boil. Cover and simmer for about 45 minutes, until the beans are tender. Add the herbs and reserved tomato and cook for a further 10 minutes. Serves 8.

Crab and shrimp bisque

Imperial/Metric
1 rasher streaky bacon
1 small onion
1 lb./450 g. tomatoes
1 pint/generous ½ litre
 chicken stock
4 oz./125 g. peeled shrimps
4 oz./125 g. crabmeat
salt and pepper
lemon juice
¼ pint/1½ dl. double cream

American
1 slice side bacon
1 small onion
1 lb. tomatoes
2½ cups chicken broth
⅔ cup peeled shrimp
½ cup crab meat
salt and pepper
lemon juice
½ cup whipping cream

Dice the bacon and fry until the fat runs. Chop the onion and fry in the bacon fat until limp. Skin and deseed the tomatoes. Add the tomato flesh and chicken stock to the onion and bacon. Simmer for 10 minutes. Sieve or liquidise in a blender. Return to the saucepan and stir in the shrimps and crabmeat. Add salt, pepper and lemon juice to taste. Reheat, then stir in the cream. This soup may be served hot or cold.

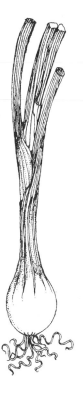

Summer lettuce soup

Imperial/Metric
1 large lettuce
4 spring onions
1 oz./25 g. butter
2 tablespoons flour
1 pint/generous ½ litre
  milk
1 teaspoon salt
¼ teaspoon pepper
¼ teaspoon dried tarragon
1 egg yolk
1 tablespoon chopped mint

American
1 large lettuce
4 green onions
2 tablespoons butter
2 tablespoons all-purpose
  flour
2½ cups milk
1 teaspoon salt
¼ teaspoon pepper
¼ teaspoon dried tarragon
1 egg yolk
1 tablespoon chopped mint

Wash the lettuce and shred it. Chop the spring onions. Melt the butter in a saucepan. Add the lettuce and onion and cook gently for 5 minutes. Stir in the flour. Cook for 2-3 minutes. Remove from the heat and gradually add the milk and seasonings. Return to the heat and simmer covered, for 30 minutes. Liquidise in a blender, or sieve. Pour into a clean saucepan. Whisk in the egg yolk. Reheat gently but do not allow to boil. Pour into hot soup bowls and garnish with chopped mint.

Rhubarb soup

Imperial/Metric
1 lb./450 g. rhubarb
1½ pints/scant 1 litre water
1 cinnamon stick
2 thin slices lemon
6 oz./175 g. sugar
2 tablespoons cornflour
1 egg yolk
¼ pint/1½ dl. double cream

American
1 lb. rhubarb
3¾ cups water
1 cinnamon stick
2 thin slices lemon
¾ cup sugar
2 tablespoons cornstarch
1 egg yolk
½ cup whipping cream

Cut the rhubarb into 1 inch/2 cm. pieces. Simmer in the water until tender. Drain through a sieve and discard the pulp. Simmer the rhubarb juice with the cinnamon stick, lemon slices and sugar until the sugar dissolves. Mix the cornflour with a little cold water and stir into the soup. Bring to the boil and simmer for 5 minutes, stirring continuously. Remove the cinnamon stick and lemon slices. Combine the egg yolk and double cream; stir into the hot soup. Heat through, but do not allow to boil. Serve hot with Melba toast.

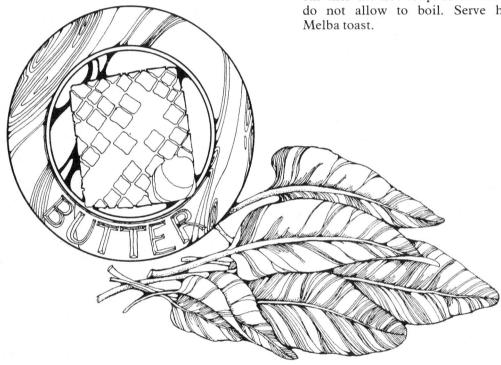

 # Sorrel stuffed eggs

Imperial/Metric
4 eggs
2 oz./50 g. sorrel leaves
1 oz./25 g. butter
3 tablespoons cream cheese
1 teaspoon grated onion
salt and pepper
8 peeled shrimps
watercress leaves

American
4 eggs
2 bunches sorrel
2 tablespoons butter
3 tablespoons cream cheese
1 teaspoon minced onion
salt and pepper
8 peeled shrimp
watercress leaves

Hard boil the eggs, shell and cut in half. Scoop out the yolk. Cook the sorrel in the butter in a tightly covered pan for about 8 minutes, or until tender. Drain and chop very finely. Mash the cooked egg yolks with the sorrel and cream cheese. Beat in the minced onion and seasonings. Spoon the mixture into the egg white halves. Top each egg half with a shrimp for garnish. Arrange on a bed of watercress leaves. Serve with thinly sliced brown bread and butter.

Herb tartlets

Imperial/Metric
12 oz./350 g. shortcrust
  pastry
5 oz./150 g. curd cheese
2 eggs, beaten
1 tablespoon chopped
  chives
salt and pepper

American
¾ lb. basic pie dough
1¼ cups farmer cheese
2 eggs, beaten
1 tablespoon chopped
  chives
salt and pepper

Roll out the pastry thinly, cut out circles with a fluted biscuit cutter and use to line 8 patty tins. Bake blind in a moderately hot oven (375°F, 190°C, Gas Mark 5) for 10 minutes. Meanwhile, beat the cheese until smooth, then gradually add the eggs, chives and seasoning to taste. Divide the filling between the 8 tartlet cases and return to the oven for 20 minutes, until well risen and brown. Serve hot as an hors d'oeuvre, to be followed by a clear soup.

Deep-fried almond prawns

Imperial/Metric
1 lb./450 g. fresh prawns
2 oz./50 g. plain flour
¼ teaspoon white pepper
¼ teaspoon ground
  coriander
2 eggs
1 tablespoon cooking oil
½ teaspoon soy sauce
3 oz./75 g. ground
  almonds

American
1 lb. large shrimp
½ cup all-purpose flour
¼ teaspoon white pepper
¼ teaspoon ground
  coriander
2 eggs
1 tablespoon cooking oil
½ teaspoon soy sauce
¾ cup ground almonds

Shell the prawns, leaving the tail, and remove the back veins. Mix the flour, pepper and coriander. Dip each prawn into the flour mixture. Beat the eggs lightly and mix with the oil and soy sauce. Dip the flour-coated prawns into the egg mixture, and then into the ground almonds. Fry in hot deep fat for 3 minutes. Serve with lemon wedges or soy sauce.

 # Smoked cod's roe cream

Imperial/Metric
3 slices white bread
2 fl. oz./50 ml. water
8 oz./225 g. smoked cod's
  roe
1 small onion, grated
freshly ground black pepper
juice of 1 lemon
4 tablespoons oil
4 tablespoons double
  cream
few black olives

American
3 slices white bread
¼ cup water
½ lb. smoked cod's roe
1 small onion, grated
freshly ground black pepper
juice of 1 lemon
⅓ cup oil
¼ cup heavy cream
few black olives

Remove crusts from the bread and soak in the water. Skin the cod's roe and pound with the onion and soaked bread, pepper to taste, the lemon juice and oil to make a smooth paste. Gradually beat in the cream. Spoon into 4 small ramekin dishes and chill. Garnish with halved and stoned olives and serve with Melba toast.

Chilled fresh crab cocktails

Imperial/Metric
1 fresh crab
1 lettuce, shredded
4 inch/10 cm. length
 cucumber
2 tablespoons French
 dressing
4 tablespoons double
 cream
4 tablespoons mayonnaise

American
1 fresh crab
1 lettuce, shredded
4 inch length cucumber
2 tablespoons Italian
 dressing
¼ cup whipping cream
¼ cup mayonnaise

Boil the crab for 20 minutes, and cool. Place crab on its back, remove large and small claws. Remove 'flaps' or 'aprons'. Hold shell firmly in left hand, use right hand to pull out body from the shell. Remove gills, intestines and stomach. Carefully scrape out brown meat from shell discarding 'fingers' which are inedible. Crack large claws, remove white flesh, and chop roughly.

Half-fill cocktail glasses with shredded lettuce. Mix brown and white crab meats together. Cut the cucumber into fine dice, toss in the dressing and arrange on the lettuce in the centre, with crab meat round the edge. Mix the cream and mayonnaise together, use to mask the crab meat and place one small claw curved over the centre of each glass. Serve chilled.

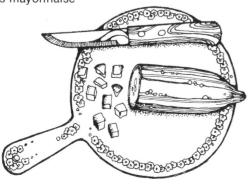

Crab imperial

Imperial/Metric	American
1 green pepper	1 green pepper
½ oz./15 g. butter	1 tablespoon butter
1 canned red pimiento	1 canned red pimiento
3 tablespoons mayonnaise	3 tablespoons mayonnaise
1 teaspoon Worcestershire sauce	1 teaspoon Worcestershire sauce
1 teaspoon salt	1 teaspoon salt
¼ teaspoon dry mustard	¼ teaspoon dry mustard
1 lb./450 g. crab meat	1 lb. crab meat
1 tablespoon dry sherry	1 tablespoon dry sherry
1 oz./25 g. grated Cheddar cheese	¼ cup grated Cheddar cheese
½ teaspoon paprika pepper	½ teaspoon paprika pepper

Chop the green pepper finely. Sauté in the butter for 2 minutes. Cool. Chop the canned pimiento finely. Stir the green pepper, pimiento, mayonnaise, Worcestershire sauce, salt, and dry mustard into the crab meat, mixing thoroughly. Spoon the mixture into cleaned crab shells or a baking dish. Sprinkle the sherry, cheese and paprika over the crab mixture. Bake in a moderate oven (350°F, 180°C, Gas Mark 4) for 20 minutes or until heated through. Serves 6, as a hot hors d'oeuvre.

 # Salmon shell salad

Imperial/Metric	American
4 oz./125 g. small pasta shells	1 cup small pasta shells
12 oz./350 g. cooked fresh or canned salmon	¾ lb. cooked fresh or canned salmon
4 inch/10 cm. length cucumber	4 inch length cucumber
¼ pint/1½ dl. soured cream	generous ½ cup soured cream
salt and ground black pepper	salt and ground black pepper
cress and lemon slices to garnish	cress and lemon slices to garnish.

Cook the pasta shells in boiling salted water for 7 minutes, or until just tender. Drain well. Meanwhile, break up the salmon, removing any skin and bones. Chop the unpeeled cucumber and mix carefully with the fish and pasta. Season the cream with salt and pepper and stir gently into the fish mixture. Adjust the seasoning and divide the mixture between 4 scallop shells or individual dishes. Garnish with cress and lemon slices cut into the shape of butterflies. Serve with thin slices of brown bread and butter.

Spiced tomato cocktail

Imperial/Metric	**American**
1 lb./450 g. ripe tomatoes	1 lb. ripe tomatoes
1 small onion	1 small onion
1 stick celery	1 stalk celery
1 tablespoon sugar	1 tablespoon sugar
1 teaspoon salt	1 teaspoon salt
$\frac{1}{4}$ teaspoon pepper	$\frac{1}{4}$ teaspoon pepper
3 whole cloves	3 whole cloves
pinch ground ginger	dash ground ginger
2 fl. oz./50 ml. water	$\frac{1}{4}$ cup water
2 tablespoons lemon juice	2 tablespoons lemon juice
1 tablespoon white vinegar	1 tablespoon white vinegar

Chop the tomatoes, onion and celery stick. Add the remaining ingredients and simmer until the vegetables are tender. Pass through a strainer, discarding the pulp. Refrigerate the juice until serving time, or put in cubes of ice. Serve in tall glasses with curls of lemon rind hanging over the edges.

Smoked haddock pâté

Imperial/Metric	**American**
8 oz./225 g. cooked smoked haddock	$\frac{1}{2}$ lb. cooked finnan haddie
juice of $\frac{1}{2}$ lemon	juice of $\frac{1}{2}$ lemon
3 oz./75 g. cream cheese	1 package (3 oz.) cream cheese
ground black pepper	ground black pepper
2 tablespoons single cream	2 tablespoons coffee cream
4 lemon slices	4 lemon slices
4 parsley sprigs	4 parsley sprigs
2 sticks celery	2 stalks celery
2 medium carrots	2 medium carrots

Flake the haddock and pound with the lemon juice. Beat in the cream cheese until smooth. Season to taste with black pepper and beat in the cream. Divide the mixture between 4 stemmed glass dishes, each placed on a saucer. Garnish the top with lemon twists and parsley. Cut the celery sticks into 1 inch/2 cm. lengths and cut the carrots into very thin sticks. Arrange a ring of the vegetables decoratively around the base of each dish.

Main dishes

Salmon is top of the list and like other fish at this time of the year is just as delightful served cold as hot. If you prefer meat, try tender veal or duck cold in gleaming aspic for a change.

Fresh salmon puff

Imperial/Metric
1 lb./450 g. frozen puff
  pastry, defrosted
6 oz./175 g. cooked fresh
  salmon
8 oz./225 g. cooked white
  fish
½ pint/3 dl. savoury white
  sauce
4 oz./125 g. cooked rice
2 tablespoons chopped
  parsley
1 teaspoon anchovy
  essence
beaten egg to glaze
lemon wedges
sprigs of watercress

American
1 lb. puff paste
6 oz. cooked fresh salmon
½ lb. cooked white fish
1¼ cups savory white sauce
¾ cup cooked rice
3 tablespoons chopped
  parsley
1 teaspoon anchovy extract
beaten egg to glaze
lemon wedges
sprigs of watercress

Roll out the pastry to a rectangle 14 inches/35 cm. by 8 inches/20 cm. Cut triangles with 4 inch/10 cm. sides off each corner. Mix together all ingredients for the filling and place down the centre of the pastry. Fold up the sides and pointed ends of the pastry to make a neat rectangle. Brush with beaten egg and seal the edges well together. Roll out pastry trimmings and cut into strips. Plait these together and use to cover the joins in the pastry envelope. Brush all over with beaten egg and place on a damped baking sheet. Bake in a hot oven (450°F, 230°C, Gas Mark 8) for 10 minutes, then lower heat to moderately hot (375°F, 190°C, Gas Mark 5) for a further 30 minutes. Garnish with lemon wedges and sprigs of watercress.

Avocado and salmon mousse

Imperial/Metric
8 oz./200 g. cooked fresh
  or canned salmon
scant ½ oz./15 g. gelatine
2 avocado pears
½ teaspoon salt
pinch white pepper
2 teaspoons anchovy
  essence
3 tablespoons single cream
few drops green food
  colouring
2 egg whites
1 stuffed green olive and
  parsley to garnish

American
½ lb. cooked fresh or
  canned salmon
1 tablespoon unflavored
  gelatin
2 avocado pears
½ teaspoon salt
dash white pepper
2 teaspoons anchovy
  extract
3 tablespoons coffee cream
few drops green food
  coloring
2 egg whites
1 stuffed green olive and
  parsley to garnish

Drain the salmon, reserving the juice, or a little cooking liquid, remove the bones and skin and flake the flesh. Dissolve the gelatine in 3 tablespoons hot water. Cut the avocados in half lengthwise, remove the stones and skin and cut the flesh into pieces. Liquidise the avocado, salt, pepper, anchovy essence and the salmon juice in a blender, until smooth, or mash thoroughly with a fork and then beat until smooth. Place in a fairly large bowl, stir in the dissolved gelatine, the cream and the flaked salmon, adding a little green food colouring. Whisk the egg whites until just holding their shape, then using a metal spoon fold into the salmon mixture. Turn into a rinsed fish mould or ring mould and leave to set. Turn out on to a serving platter and garnish with olive slices and parsley. Serve with prawns, or a salad garnish.

29

Main Dishes

★ Barbecued salmon steaks

Imperial/Metric
4 fl. oz./100 ml. dry white wine
¼ teaspoon dried marjoram
1 teaspoon grated onion
pinch pepper
4 salmon steaks
salt

American
½ cup Californian Chablis wine
¼ teaspoon dried marjoram
1 teaspoon grated onion
dash pepper
4 salmon steaks
salt

Combine the wine, marjoram, onion and pepper and pour over salmon steaks in a shallow dish. Refrigerate for several hours, turning the salmon once or twice. Drain well. Grill until the fish flakes easily with a fork, turning once. Sprinkle with salt as the salmon cooks.

Halibut steaks with turmeric cream

Imperial/Metric
6 oz./175 g. long grain
  rice
1 teaspoon powdered
  turmeric
2 drops yellow food
  colouring
2 small lemons
4 halibut steaks
salt and pepper
4 inch/10 cm. length
  cucumber
1 oz./25 g. butter
$\frac{1}{4}$ pint/1$\frac{1}{2}$ dl. double cream
4 sprigs of mint

American
$\frac{3}{4}$ cup long grain rice
1 teaspoon powdered
  turmeric
2 drops yellow food
  coloring
2 small lemons
4 halibut steaks
salt and pepper
4 inch length cucumber
2 tablespoons butter
generous $\frac{1}{2}$ cup whipping
  cream
4 sprigs of mint

Cook the rice in boiling salted water, with half the turmeric and the food colouring if liked. Drain and keep warm. Meanwhile, grate the zest from one lemon and squeeze the juice. Reserve one teaspoon of lemon juice and use the remaining juice to poach the fish steaks, plus just sufficient water to cover and seasoning to taste, for about 10 minutes, until tender enough for the flesh to separate easily from the bone. Drain the fish and keep hot. Slice the cucumber thickly, cut each slice into four and toss in the melted butter until limp. Cut the second lemon into quarters. Whip the cream with the remaining turmeric, salt, pepper and a few drops of reserved lemon juice. Arrange the fish steaks on a warm serving dish and pipe rosettes of seasoned cream down the centres. Sprinkle with grated lemon zest and place the cooked cucumber in the centre. Use the lemon quarters as dividers. Divide the rice between 4 individual dishes, and garnish with the tops of the mint sprigs. Chop the leaves and sprinkle over the cucumber. Serve at once before the cream melts.

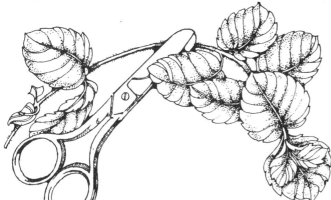

Mackerel in foil parcels

Imperial/Metric
4 mackerel
1 oz./25 g. butter
juice and grated zest of
   1 lemon
1 onion, sliced in thin
   rings
1 tablespoon chopped
   parsley
lemon wedges to garnish

American
4 mackerel
2 tablespoons butter
juice and grated rind of
   1 lemon
1 onion, sliced in thin
   rings
1 tablespoon chopped
   parsley
lemon wedges to garnish

Clean the fish and cut off the heads and tails. Place each fish on a piece of foil about 8 inches/20 cm. square, or to suit the size of the fish. Spread a little butter inside each fish, with a few drops of lemon juice. Top with a few onion rings and a little grated lemon zest. Sprinkle with chopped parsley and enclose the fish in the foil to make firm watertight parcels. Place on a baking sheet and cook in a moderate oven (350°F, 180°C, Gas Mark 4) for 30-35 minutes. Serve from the parcels, and garnish with lemon wedges.

Cod steaks with mushroom cream sauce

Imperial/Metric
1 lb./450 g. button
   mushrooms
2 oz./50 g. butter
1 teaspoon oil
12 fl. oz./3½ dl. milk
3 bay leaves
2 chicken stock cubes
1 small onion, chopped
4 cod steaks
2 tablespoons flour
1 teaspoon lemon juice
salt and pepper
7 tablespoons single cream

American
1 lb. button mushrooms
¼ cup butter
1 teaspoon oil
1½ cups milk
3 bay leaves
2 chicken bouillon cubes
1 small onion, chopped
4 cod steaks
2 tablespoons flour
1 teaspoon lemon juice
salt and pepper
½ cup half-and-half

Remove and chop the mushroom stalks. Slice the mushroom caps. Cook gently, covered, in about one third of the butter with the oil until limp. Meanwhile, bring the milk to the boil with the bay leaves, stock cubes and onion. Strain the milk and use to poach the fish steaks until cooked. In a separate pan, melt the remaining butter and stir in the flour. Cook, stirring, for 2 minutes then gradually add the strained liquid from cooking the fish. Whisk over low heat until the sauce is smooth and simmer for 2 minutes. Add the mushrooms, lemon juice, and extra seasoning if necessary. Just before serving stir in the cream and reheat but do not allow to boil. Place the fish steaks on a hot serving dish and spoon over the sauce.

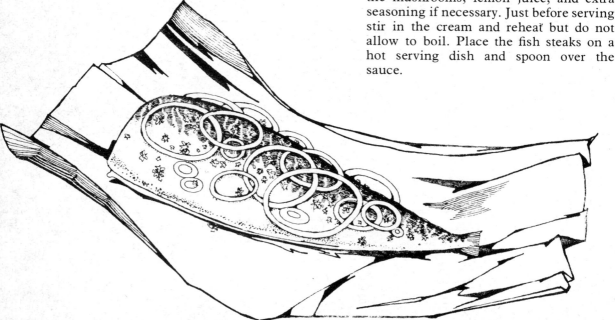

Piquant veal escalopes

Imperial/Metric
4 escalopes of veal
seasoned flour for coating
3 oz./75 g. butter
6 spring onions, chopped
1 lemon, sliced
2 teaspoons dried rosemary
salt and freshly ground
　black pepper
¼ teaspoon Tabasco pepper
　sauce
¼ pint/1½ dl. dry vermouth
1 tablespoon chopped
　parsley

American
4 escalopes of veal
seasoned flour for coating
6 tablespoons butter
6 scallions, chopped
1 lemon, sliced
2 teaspoons dried rosemary
salt and freshly ground
　black pepper
¼ teaspoon Tabasco pepper
　sauce
½ cup dry vermouth
1 tablespoon chopped
　parsley

Bat out the escalopes thinly and cut each in half. Dust with seasoned flour. Quickly fry them in 2 oz./50 g. of the butter until golden. Remove and keep warm. Fry the white part of the spring onions in the remaining butter until soft. Replace the veal and add the lemon slices, rosemary, seasoning, Tabasco, vermouth and green part of the spring onions. Cook for a further 2-3 minutes. Arrange on a serving dish and garnish with the chopped parsley.

Caribbean stew

Imperial/Metric
8 oz./225 g. red kidney
  beans
1½ lb./675 g. collar or
  forehock bacon
1 green pepper
1 large onion
1 oz./25 g. butter
¾ pint/4 dl. water
3 tablespoons tomato
  ketchup
1 teaspoon Tabasco pepper
  sauce
pinch dried oregano
8 oz./225 g. French beans
1 tablespoon cornflour

American
1 cup red kidney beans
1½ lb. collar or forehock
  bacon
1 green pepper
1 large onion
2 tablespoons butter
2 cups water
3 tablespoons tomato
  catsup
1 teaspoon Tabasco pepper
  sauce
dash dried oregano
½ lb. green beans
1 tablespoon cornstarch

Put the kidney beans and the bacon into separate basins, cover with water and leave overnight. Remove rind and fat from bacon, and cut the meat into 1 inch/ 2 cm. cubes. Place in a saucepan, cover with cold water and bring to the boil, then drain. Deseed and chop the green pepper and chop the onion. Gently fry these in the butter until just tender, then add the bacon and drained kidney beans. Cook for one minute, then stir in the water, ketchup, Tabasco sauce and oregano. Cover and simmer for 1 hour. Cut the French beans into 1 inch/2 cm. lengths and add to the pan. Bring to the boil, cover and simmer gently for a further half hour, or until bacon and kidney beans are tender. Blend the cornflour with a little cold water, and stir into stew. Bring back to the boil, stirring constantly, until the mixture thickens. Cook for a further 2 minutes.

Lamb cutlets with pawpaw salad

Imperial/Metric
1 pawpaw
12 spring onions
8 lamb cutlets
2 tablespoons oil
1 oz./25 g. butter
salt and pepper
1 teaspoon chopped mint

American
1 pawpaw
12 scallions
8 lamb cutlets
3 tablespoons oil
2 tablespoons butter
salt and pepper
1 teaspoon chopped mint

Cut the pawpaw in half, remove the seeds and skin and cut the flesh into ¼ inch/½ cm. cubes. Trim the onions, leaving about 2 inches/4 cm. of the green top. Brush the cutlets on both sides with the oil and grill under moderate heat for about 10 minutes, turning once. Meanwhile, melt the butter in a shallow pan, add the pawpaw, onions and seasonings. Cover and simmer for 5-10 minutes until the cutlets are cooked. Place the pawpaw mixture on a serving dish, sprinkle with chopped mint and surround with the cutlets.

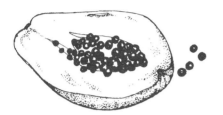

Steak with apple rice

Imperial/Metric
1 pint/generous ½ litre
   water
salt
strip of lemon rind
1 teaspoon oil
1 tablespoon sugar
8 oz./225 g. long grain rice
1 lb./450 g. apples
pinch ground cinnamon
4 rump steaks or 8 frozen
   steaklets
1 oz./25 g. butter

American
2½ cups water
salt
strip of lemon rind
1 teaspoon oil
1 tablespoon sugar
½ lb. long grain rice
1 lb. apples
dash ground cinnamon
4 rump steaks or 8 frozen
   steaklets
2 tablespoons butter

Bring the water, salt, lemon rind, oil and sugar to the boil. Add the rice and the peeled, cored and sliced apples. Season with cinnamon. Stir, lower heat to simmer, cover and cook for 15 minutes, or until the rice and apples are tender and the liquid absorbed. Fry the steaks or steaklets in the butter and serve on a bed of apple rice.

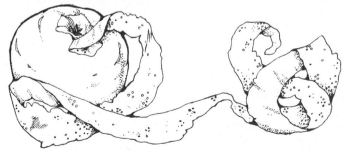

Pork with summer cabbage

Imperial/Metric
1½ lb./675 g. cabbage
1 large onion
1 clove of garlic
1 oz./25 g. butter
4 pork chops
salt and freshly ground
  black pepper
½ pint/3 dl. dry cider
4 tablespoons double cream
2 oz./50 g. Cheddar cheese,
  grated

American
1½ lb. cabbage
1 large onion
1 clove of garlic
2 tablespoons butter
4 pork chops
salt and freshly ground
  black pepper
1¼ cups dry cider
⅓ cup whipping cream
½ cup grated Cheddar
  cheese

Finely shred the cabbage and cook in boiling salted water for 2 minutes. Drain and turn into a bowl. Finely chop the onion and crush the garlic. Melt half the butter in a frying pan, add the onion and garlic and fry gently for 10 minutes. Add to the cabbage, mix lightly and turn half of it into the bottom of an ovenproof casserole. Melt the remaining butter in the frying pan, season the chops with salt and pepper and fry quickly on both sides until golden brown. Remove from the pan and place on the cabbage in the casserole. Cover with the remaining cabbage. Pour the cider into the frying pan and boil over a moderate heat until reduced to about 4 tablespoons. Remove from the heat, stir in the cream, then pour over the cabbage. Cover and bake in a moderate oven (350°F, 180°C, Gas Mark 4) for 25 minutes. Remove from the oven, sprinkle the cheese on top and bake uncovered for a further 20 minutes, or until the cheese is golden brown.

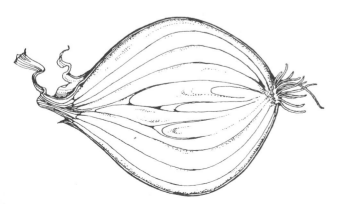

37

☆ Southern fried chicken with concasse of tomatoes

Imperial/Metric
4 southern fried chicken
  portions, defrosted
oil for frying
8 oz./225 g. ribbon noodles
3 oz./75 g. butter
salt and pepper
8 oz./225 g. button
  mushrooms
2 teaspoons lemon juice
8 oz./225 g. courgettes
1 tablespoon oil
concasse:
1 lb./450 g. tomatoes
1 small onion, grated
2 tablespoons oil
1 tablespoon vinegar
1 teaspoon ground nutmeg
1 teaspoon sugar
salt and ground black
  pepper

American
4 southern fried chicken
  portions, defrosted
oil for frying
½ lb. ribbon noodles
6 tablespoons butter
salt and pepper
½ lb. button mushrooms
2 teaspoons lemon juice
½ lb. small zucchini
1 tablespoon oil
concasse:
1 lb. tomatoes
¼ cup grated onion
2 tablespoons oil
1 tablespoon vinegar
1 teaspoon ground nutmeg
1 teaspoon sugar
salt and ground black
  pepper

Deep fry the chicken joints in hot oil as instructions on the pack. Cook the noodles in boiling salted water for about 12 minutes, until just tender. Rinse in hot water and toss with 1 oz./25 g. of the butter, salt and pepper to taste. Sprinkle the mushrooms with lemon juice and slice the courgettes. Heat together the remaining butter and the oil and use to fry the mushrooms and courgettes until light brown. Meanwhile, make the concasse. Skin the tomatoes, remove seeds and chop the flesh. Mix with all other ingredients and place in a saucepan. Bring to the boil and simmer until the sauce thickens slightly. Arrange chicken portions on a bed of noodles, place the courgettes and mushrooms round the chicken and pour over the concasse of tomatoes.

Rabbit in vermouth with fennel

Imperial/Metric
4 small heads fennel
1 young rabbit, jointed
2 tablespoons seasoned
   flour
3 oz./75 g. butter
2 medium onions, chopped
3 fl. oz./1 dl. dry vermouth
1 bay leaf
½ pint/3 dl. white stock
salt and pepper.

American
4 small heads fennel
1 young rabbit, jointed
2 tablespoons seasoned
   flour
6 tablespoons butter
2 medium onions, chopped
⅓ cup dry vermouth
1 bay leaf
1¼ cups white stock
salt and pepper.

Trim and halve the fennel. Remove and chop outer leaves. Turn the rabbit joints in the seasoned flour. Melt half the butter and use to fry the chopped onion and fennel leaves gently until limp. Add the rabbit joints and sauté, turning frequently, until golden brown on all sides. Add the vermouth, and allow to cook for 2 minutes, stirring constantly. Add the bay leaf and pour in the stock. Bring to the boil, reduce heat, cover and simmer for about 40 minutes, until the rabbit is tender. Meanwhile, turn the fennel halves in the remaining butter until well coated. Season to taste and add just enough water to cover. Cook over low heat, covered, for about 20 minutes, until tender. Remove lid and increase heat to make fennel halves golden on the outside. Serve with the rabbit.

 # Chicken livers in Madeira sauce

Imperial Metric
5 oz./150 g. long grain rice
1 teaspoon salt
12 oz./350 g. chicken livers
flour for coating
1 apple
1½ oz./40 g. butter
sauce:
1 oz./25 g. butter
1 oz./25 g. flour
¾ pint/4½ dl. strong beef
   stock
4 tablespoons Madeira

American
¾ cup long grain rice
1 teaspoon salt
¾ lb. chicken livers
flour for coating
1 apple
3 tablespoons butter
sauce:
2 tablespoons butter
¼ cup all purpose flour
2 cups strong beef broth
⅓ cup Madeira

Cook the rice in 1¾ pints/1 litre/4½ cups boiling water with the salt for 12-15 minutes. Drain and keep hot. Meanwhile, make the sauce. Melt the butter, stir in the flour and cook, stirring, until golden brown. Gradually add the stock and bring to the boil, stirring constantly. Add the Madeira and cook for 5 minutes to reduce the sauce slightly. Coat the chicken livers lightly with flour and core and slice the apple. Melt the butter and use to fry the livers and apple slices for about 5 minutes, until livers are firm and just cooked through. Serve the livers with the hot rice and pour the sauce over. Garnish with apple slices. Serves 3.

Orange basted chicken with baby beetroots

Imperial/Metric	American
3 lb./1½ kg. chicken	3 lb. chicken
salt and pepper	salt and pepper
2 tablespoons frozen orange concentrate	2 tablespoons frozen orange concentrate
1 tablespoon soy sauce	1 tablespoon soy sauce
2 tablespoons boiling water	2 tablespoons boiling water
1 lb./450 g. baby beetroots	1 lb. baby beets
béchamel sauce:	béchamel sauce:
1 small carrot	1 small carrot
1 small onion	1 small onion
1 pint/generous ½ litre milk	2½ cups milk
2 peppercorns	2 peppercorns
1 bay leaf	1 bay leaf
pinch ground mace	dash ground mace
2 oz./50 g. butter	¼ cup butter
2 oz./50 g. flour	½ cup all purpose flour
salt and pepper	salt and pepper

Sprinkle the chicken with salt and pepper and place in a small roasting tin. Mix together the orange juice concentrate, soy sauce and boiling water. Roast the chicken in a moderately hot oven (400°F, 200°C, Gas Mark 6) for 1 hour and 20 minutes, basting frequently with the orange soy sauce after the first 20 minutes. Meanwhile, cook the beetroots and make the béchamel sauce. Trim the beetroots and cook in boiling salted water for about 20 minutes, until tender. To make the sauce, roughly chop the carrot and onion and place in a saucepan with the milk, peppercorns, bay leaf and mace. Bring to the boil and allow to stand for 10 minutes. In a clean saucepan melt the butter, stir in the flour and cook for 3 minutes without browning. Gradually strain in the flavoured milk and bring to the boil, stirring all the time, until the sauce is smooth and thick. Season to taste with salt and pepper. Place the chicken on a hot serving dish. Peel the beetroots, place them in a hot vegetable dish and pour the sauce over them.

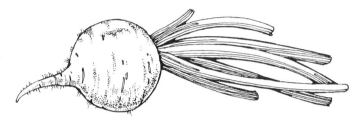

Chicken in tomato rechauffé

Imperial/Metric	American
12 oz./350 g. cooked chicken	12 oz. cooked chicken
1 large onion	1 large onion
4 oz./125 g. celery	1 cup diced celery
8 oz./225 g. tomatoes	3 medium tomatoes
1½ oz./40 g. butter	3 tablespoons butter
1 teaspoon sugar	1 teaspoon granulated sugar
1 chicken stock cube	1 chicken bouillon cube
½ oz./15 g. cornflour	1 tablespoon cornstarch
salt and pepper	salt and pepper
1 large slice white bread	1 large slice white bread

Dice the chicken, finely chop the onion and celery and chop the tomatoes. Melt 1 oz./25 g. of the butter, add the onion and celery and fry over moderate heat for about 5 minutes until pale golden brown. Add the sugar, chopped tomato and stock cube dissolved in ½ pint/3 dl./ 1¼ cups boiling water. Bring to the boil, stir well, add the chicken, bring back to the boil. Meanwhile moisten the cornflour with 2 tablespoons cold water, add to the pan, and cook stirring constantly for about 3 minutes, until thickened. Add salt and pepper to taste. Cut the bread into neat dice. Melt the remaining butter and use to fry the bread until golden brown. Serve the chicken mixture sprinkled with the fried bread croûtons.

 # Turkey and apricot pilau

Imperial/Metric
1 tablespoon oil
1 clove garlic, crushed
1 onion, chopped
salt and pepper
pinch ground ginger
8 oz./225 g. long grain rice
1 lb./450 g. cooked turkey
1 pint/generous ½ litre
    chicken stock
2 oz./50 g. raisins
8 oz./225 g. apricots
1 tablespoon soy sauce
1 teaspoon sherry

American
1 tablespoon oil
1 clove garlic, crushed
1 onion, chopped
salt and pepper
dash ground ginger
½ lb. long grain rice
1 lb. cooked turkey
2½ cups chicken broth
½ cup seedless raisins
½ lb. apricots
1 tablespoon soy sauce
1 teaspoon sherry

Heat the oil and use to fry the garlic and onion until soft. Add salt, pepper, ground ginger and rice and fry quickly. Cut the turkey into cubes and add to the pan with the stock and raisins. Lower heat to simmer, cover and cook for 10 minutes. Halve the apricots, remove the stones and simmer in a little boiling water until just tender. Drain the apricots, add to the rice and continue cooking for a further 5 minutes. Stir in the soy sauce and sherry. Serve with a green salad.

Duck in vinegar jelly

Imperial/Metric
1 duck (4-4½ lb./about 2kg.)
2 chicken stock cubes
2 bay leaves
2 cloves
4 peppercorns
1 egg white and shell
½ oz./15 g. gelatine
6 tablespoons vinegar
salt and pepper
¼ pint/1½ dl. thick
　mayonnaise
cucumber slices to garnish

American
1 duck (4-4½ lb.)
2 chicken bouillon cubes
2 bay leaves
2 cloves
4 peppercorns
1 egg white and shell
2 envelopes unflavored
　gelatin
½ cup vinegar
salt and pepper
generous ½ cup thick
　mayonnaise
cucumber slices to garnish

Cook the duck in a covered casserole in sufficient water to cover with the stock cubes, bay leaves and spices, for about 1 hour, until just tender. Remove the duck, cool, and drain the juices from it back into the casserole. Bone and cut the meat into large pieces. Reheat the stock, strain and make up to 1¼ pints/7½ dl./3 cups with water if needed. Add the lightly beaten egg white and crushed shell and return to a clean saucepan. Boil until clear. Strain off the cleared stock and stir in the gelatine until dissolved. Add the vinegar, taste and adjust seasoning. Pour a little of the stock into the base of a shallow oval or rectangular mould. When set arrange a layer of duck on this, cover with stock and chill until firm. Add rest of duck meat, cover with remaining stock and chill. When set, loosen edges with a knife, dip base in hot water and turn out. Garnish with piped rosettes of mayonnaise and cucumber triangles. Serve with a fresh tomato salad.

Tongue and asparagus custard

Imperial/Metric
¾ pint/4½ dl. milk
4 eggs
1 teaspoon salt
freshly ground black pepper
½ teaspoon celery seed
½ teaspoon dried dill weed
    (optional)
1 lb. cooked asparagus
    spears
4 oz./125 g. can ox tongue

American
2 cups milk
4 eggs
1 teaspoon salt
freshly ground black pepper
½ teaspoon celery seed
½ teaspoon dried dill weed
    (optional)
1 lb. cooked asparagus
    spears
4 oz. can ox tongue

Beat the milk, eggs, seasoning and herbs together. Reserve 6 asparagus spears for garnish. Chop the remainder and the tongue and add to the custard mixture. Pour into a well greased flan dish and bake in a moderately hot oven (375°F, 190°C, Gas Mark 5) for 35 minutes. Serve hot garnished with the reserved asparagus spears.

Spanish rice and sausage salad

Imperial/Metric
1 chicken stock cube
¾ pint/4½ dl. boiling water
1 green pepper
1 large onion
2 oz./50 g. butter
8 oz./225 g. long grain rice
¼ teaspoon ground
    cinnamon
¼ teaspoon powdered
    saffron
salt and ground black
    pepper
1 lb./450 g. chipolata
    sausages
4 slices fresh pineapple
endive to garnish

American
1 chicken bouillon cube
2 cups boiling water
1 green pepper
1 large onion
¼ cup butter
½ lb. long grain rice
¼ teaspoon ground
    cinnamon
¼ teaspoon powdered
    saffron
salt and ground black
    pepper
1 lb. thin pork links
4 slices fresh pineapple
green salad to
    garnish

Dissolve the stock cube in the boiling water. Deseed and slice the pepper and finely slice the onion. Melt the butter and use to fry the pepper and onion slices until softened. Stir in the rice and fry until it begins to turn golden. Add sufficient stock to cover the rice and mix in the spices. Continue cooking slowly, adding more stock as required and stirring frequently, until the rice is cooked. Season to taste with salt and pepper. Meanwhile, grill the sausages and pineapple slices and keep hot. Serve the rice piled up in a warm serving dish with the sausages and pineapple on top. Garnish with green salad.

Chicken with mushroom wine sauce

Imperial/Metric
4 chicken breast portions
2 teaspoons oil
1 small onion, chopped
1 stick celery, sliced
$\frac{1}{4}$ pint/1$\frac{1}{2}$ dl. white wine
$\frac{1}{4}$ pint/1$\frac{1}{2}$ dl. water
1 chicken stock cube
$\frac{1}{2}$ teaspoon salt
$\frac{1}{4}$ teaspoon dried savory
pinch dried thyme
few drops Worcestershire
   sauce
1 teaspoon lemon juice
4 oz./125 g. mushrooms,
   sliced
2 teaspoons cornflour
1 tablespoon chopped
   canned red pimiento
1 tablespoon chopped
   parsley.

American
4 chicken breast portions
2 teaspoons oil
1 small onion, chopped
1 stalk celery, sliced
generous $\frac{1}{2}$ cup Californian
   Sauterne
generous $\frac{1}{2}$ cup water
1 chicken bouillon cube
$\frac{1}{2}$ teaspoon salt
$\frac{1}{4}$ teaspoon dried savory
dash dried thyme
few drops Worcestershire
   sauce
1 teaspoon lemon juice
1$\frac{1}{2}$ cups sliced mushrooms
2 teaspoons cornstarch
1 tablespoon chopped
   canned red pimiento
1 tablespoon chopped
   parsley

Remove skin and bone from chicken breasts. Heat the oil and use to sauté the onion and celery lightly. Add the wine, water, stock cube, salt, herbs, Worcestershire sauce and lemon juice and bring to the boil. Add the chicken breasts, cover and cook gently for about 20 minutes, until chicken is tender. Add the mushrooms and cook for a further 5 minutes. Moisten the cornflour with a little cold water, add to the pan and bring to the boil, stirring constantly, until sauce is slightly thickened and clear. Stir in the pimiento, sprinkle with parsley and serve with hot green beans.

Fiesta kebabs

Imperial/Metric
16 chipolata sausages
1 melon
2 slices fresh pineapple
1 canned red pimiento
1 green pepper
4 oz./125 g. Cheddar
  cheese, cubed
8 cocktail onions
8 slices cucumber
sprigs of parsley or mint

American
16 thin pork links
1 melon
2 slices fresh pineapple
1 canned red pimiento
1 green pepper
$\frac{1}{4}$ lb. Cheddar cheese,
  cubed
8 cocktail onions
8 slices cucumber
sprigs of parsley or mint

Grill the sausages until evenly browned. Cut the base off the melon and discard the pips. Scoop out the flesh into neat balls, and place the melon, cut side down, on a serving dish. Cut the pineapple and pimiento into chunks and deseed and cut the pepper into wedges. Thread the sausages, melon balls and other ingredients on long kebab skewers, alternating the colours attractively. Push the skewers well into the melon and garnish the tops with sprigs of parsley or mint. Surround the base of the melon with crushed ice.

Lamb cutlets in aspic

Imperial/Metric
6 small lamb cutlets
salt and black pepper
2 oz./50 g. butter, melted
$\frac{1}{2}$ pint/3 dl. liquid aspic
  jelly
1 tablespoon dry sherry
6 mint leaves
1 lemon
few lettuce leaves
1 cooked carrot, sliced

American
6 small lamb cutlets
salt and black pepper
$\frac{1}{4}$ cup butter, melted
$1\frac{1}{4}$ cups liquid aspic
1 tablespoon dry sherry
6 mint leaves
1 lemon
few lettuce leaves
1 cooked carrot, sliced

Season the cutlets with salt and black pepper. Brush with melted butter and cook under a hot grill for 3 minutes on each side. Cool. Make up the aspic jelly and stir in the sherry. Allow to cool and become syrupy. Place 1 mint leaf on each cutlet and coat several times with aspic jelly to build up a shiny glaze. Cover cutlet bones with paper frills. Thinly slice the lemon and arrange a bed of lettuce leaves on a serving dish. Place each cutlet on a circle of lemon topped with a carrot slice. Serve very cold. Serves 3.

Jellied veal

Imperial/Metric
2 lb./1 kg. pie veal
2 tablespoons oil
sprig of rosemary
sprig of thyme
1 bay leaf
salt and pepper
½ pint/3 dl. water
½ pint/3 dl. dry white wine
6 small carrots, sliced
1 egg white and shell
aspic jelly crystals to set
  1 pint/generous ½ litre
  liquid stock
2 tomatoes, quartered
sprigs of parsley

American
2 lb. pie veal
2 tablespoons oil
sprig of rosemary
sprig of thyme
1 bay leaf
salt and pepper
1¼ cups water
1¼ cups dry white wine
6 small carrots, sliced
1 egg white and shell
2½ cups liquid aspic,
  made with veal stock
2 tomatoes, quartered
sprigs of parsley

Cut the meat into large dice. Toss in the hot oil to seal. Add the herbs, salt, pepper, water and wine and cook, covered, over gentle heat for 45 minutes. Add the carrots and cook for a further 15 minutes. Remove and reserve the meat and carrots. Strain the remaining stock and bring to the boil with the lightly beaten egg white and the shell. When completely clear, strain off. Add the aspic jelly crystals dissolved in 4 tablespoons hot water and if necessary make up to 1 pint/generous ½ litre/2½ cups with more water. Pour a little stock into the base of an 8 inch/20 cm. mould or cake tin. When set, arrange carrot rings decoratively round base and sides, add half the meat and pour in half the stock. Chill until firm. Add the remaining meat, carrots and stock and chill until set. Loosen edges with a knife, dip base of mould into hot water and turn out on a serving dish. Decorate with tomato wedges and parsley sprigs.

Sausage and corn barbecue

Imperial/Metric
2 lb./1 kg. sausages
4 mild onions
barbecue sauce:
12 oz./350 g. ripe tomatoes
2½ fl. oz./65 ml. cider or
   tarragon vinegar
2 tablespoons tomato
   ketchup
1 tablespoon Worcester-
   shire sauce
2 bay leaves
1 clove garlic, chopped
3 tablespoons grated onion
3 sticks celery, chopped
½ lemon, sliced
1 tablespoon brown sugar
½ pint/3 dl. water
salt and pepper

American
2 lb. pork links
4 mild onions
barbecue sauce:
¾ lb. ripe tomatoes
⅓ cup cider or tarragon
   vinegar
3 tablespoons tomato
   catsup
1 tablespoon Worcester-
   shire sauce
2 bay leaves
1 clove garlic, chopped
3 tablespoons grated onion
3 stalks celery, chopped
½ lemon, sliced
1 tablespoon brown sugar
1¼ cups water
salt and pepper

First make the barbecue sauce. Peel the tomatoes and chop roughly. Place in a saucepan with all the other ingredients and bring to the boil. Cover and simmer gently for 30 minutes. Remove the bay leaves and lemon slices and adjust seasoning. Thread the sausages on long skewers with wedges of onion in between. Roast over a charcoal grill, turning frequently, until rich golden brown all over. Serve with hot crusty rolls, barbecue sauce and Indian style corn on the cob. Serves 8.

 # Indian style corn on the cob

Imperial/Metric
Allow 1 corn cob and 1 oz./
   25 g. butter per person
salt and pepper

American
Allow 1 corn cob and
   2 tablespoons butter per
   person
salt and pepper

Pull back the husks of each cob and remove the silky threads. Spread with softened butter, season with salt and pepper and re-fold husk leaves over cob. Thread each cob on a separate skewer and roast over charcoal, turning frequently. When the husks char, remove and cook the cobs until kernels are just golden. Serve on the skewers.

Avocado cheese flan

Imperial/Metric
6 oz./150 g. plain flour
2 oz./50 g. margarine
2 oz./50 g. lard
1 egg yolk
1 tablespoon cold water
filling:
1 onion
2 eggs, beaten
4 oz./125 g. Cheddar
   cheese, grated
3 tablespoons milk
2 medium avocados
salt and pepper
2 tomatoes, sliced

American
1½ cups all purpose flour
¼ cup margarine
¼ cup lard
1 egg yolk
1 tablespoon cold water
filling:
1 onion
2 eggs, beaten
1 cup grated Cheddar
   cheese
3 tablespoons milk
2 medium avocados
salt and pepper
2 tomatoes, sliced

Sieve the flour into a bowl and rub in the fats. Bind with the egg yolk and water and chill the pastry well. Roll out and use to line an 8 inch/20 cm. flan dish. Finely chop the onion and mix with the eggs, cheese and milk in a large bowl. Halve the avocados, remove the stones and dice the flesh. Stir avocado into the egg mixture and add seasoning to taste. Pour the mixture into the pastry case and top with the tomato slices. Cook in a moderately hot oven (375°F, 190°C, Gas Mark 5) for 30 minutes. Serve hot or cold.

Mushroom stuffed peppers

Imperial/Metric
4 medium green peppers
4 oz./125 g. button
  mushrooms
1 rasher lean bacon
1 oz./25 g. butter
1 small onion, chopped
4 chicken livers
1 tablespoon soft white
  breadcrumbs
sauce:
12 oz./350 g. ripe tomatoes
1 teaspoon sugar
salt and pepper
few drops Tabasco pepper
  sauce

American
4 medium green peppers
1 cup button mushrooms
1 bacon slice
2 tablespoons butter
1 small onion, chopped
4 chicken livers
1 tablespoon soft white
  bread crumbs
sauce:
¾ lb. ripe tomatoes
1 teaspoon sugar
salt and pepper
few drops Tabasco pepper
  sauce

Remove the stem ends from the peppers and scoop out the seeds. Pour boiling water over the pepper 'cases' to blanch them, leave 2-3 minutes, then drain well. Slice the mushrooms, reserving 4 for the garnish, derind and chop the bacon. Cook the chopped bacon in a frying pan over moderate heat until the fat runs, add the butter, onion, mushrooms and chicken livers. Cook until livers are just firm. Remove the 4 whole mushrooms and keep warm. Remove and chop the livers finely. Return to the pan with the breadcrumbs and stir until the breadcrumbs begin to turn colour. Divide the filling between the 4 pepper cases, and arrange upright in an ovenproof baking dish. To make the sauce, chop the tomatoes and place in a pan with the sugar, seasoning and Tabasco. Cook over moderate heat until thickened, about 10 minutes. Sieve and pour round the peppers in the dish. Spoon a little tomato mixture over the stuffing, cover with foil and bake in a moderate oven (350°F, 180°C, Gas Mark 4) for 35 minutes. Uncover and garnish with the reserved mushrooms. Serve with fluffy boiled rice.

Peach toasts

Imperial/Metric
4 large slices white bread
4 slices ham
2 ripe peaches
4 thin slices Gouda cheese
cayenne pepper

American
4 large slices white bread
4 slices ham
2 ripe peaches
4 thin slices Dutch cheese
cayenne pepper

Remove crusts if liked, and toast the bread lightly. Place a slice of ham, trimmed to fit, on each piece of toast. Arrange wedges of freshly peeled and stoned peaches on this. Cover with thin slices of Gouda cheese, also trimmed to fit, sprinkle with cayenne pepper and place under a hot grill until the cheese begins to melt and bubble. Serve at once with a fresh green salad, or a bowl of watercress sprigs.

Vegetables and salads

What a pleasure it is to serve a greater variety of vegetables, and generous portions of crisp green salads at a mere fraction of the winter cost. By combining cheese and fruit with savoury dressings you can turn even the simplest salad into a masterpiece, and make it a main dish.

Hot German potato salad

Imperial/Metric
2 lb./1 kg. new potatoes, cooked
¼ pint/1½ dl. strong chicken stock
¼ pint/1½ dl. mayonnaise
2 tablespoons chopped mixed fresh herbs (parsley, thyme, dill etc.)
4 large gherkins

American
2 lb. new potatoes, cooked
generous ½ cup strong chicken broth
½ cup mayonnaise
2 tablespoons chopped mixed fresh herbs (parsley, thyme, dill etc.)
4 large gherkins

Cook the potatoes in boiling salted water, drain and peel. Halve or quarter the potatoes while still warm, pour over the hot stock, then carefully fold in the mayonnaise and chopped herbs. Pile up in a serving dish or Tupperware Servalier bowl to keep hot. Serve warm, garnished with gherkin fans.
Note: To make gherkin fans, slice through lengthways about 6 times, almost to the base, and fan out.

Green bean and frankfurter salad

Imperial/Metric
12 oz./350 g. French beans
2 pairs frankfurter sausages
4 tablespoons French dressing

American
¾ lb. green beans
2 pairs frankfurters
4 tablespoons Italian dressing

Cook the beans in boiling salted water then drain and reserve the cooking liquid. Keep the beans hot. Put the sausages in the hot liquid, bring almost to the boil, cover pan and allow to stand for 5 minutes, then drain and again reserve the liquid. Slice the sausages diagonally. Mix together the French dressing and 4 tablespoons of the hot cooking liquid. Toss the hot beans and sliced sausage in this and turn into a serving dish or Tupperware Servalier bowl. Serve warm.

Cauliflower in chicken cream

Imperial/Metric
¾ pint/4 dl. milk
1 bay leaf
1 chicken stock cube
1 large cauliflower
3 oz./75 g. butter
1½ oz./40 g. flour
1 tablespoon lemon juice
2 oz./50 g. Lancashire
   cheese, grated
4 tablespoons double
   cream, whipped
1 tablespoon oil
3 oz./75 g. soft
   breadcrumbs
salt and pepper
1 teaspoon finely grated
   lemon zest

American
scant 2 cups milk
1 bay leaf
1 chicken bouillon cube
1 large cauliflower
⅓ cup butter
⅓ cup all-purpose flour
1 tablespoon lemon juice
½ cup grated cheese
⅓ cup whipping cream
1 tablespoon oil
1 cup soft bread crumbs
salt and pepper
1 teaspoon finely grated
   lemon rind

Warm the milk with the bay leaf and dissolve the stock cube in it. Allow to stand for 20 minutes. Meanwhile, cook the cauliflower whole in plenty of salted boiling water, drain and turn out carefully into a colander, invert on to a warm serving dish and keep hot. While the cauliflower is cooking, make the sauce and prepare the crumb topping. Melt half the butter, stir in the flour and cook for 2 minutes. Gradually strain in the seasoned milk, bring to the boil and whisk until smooth. Cook for 1 minute. Add the lemon juice and finally the grated cheese. As soon as the cheese is melted, stir in the cream and pour sauce over the cauliflower. Heat the remaining butter with the oil and use to fry the breadcrumbs golden brown. Season with salt and pepper, stir in the lemon zest and sprinkle over and round the cauliflower.

Israeli carrot salad

Imperial/Metric	American
4 large carrots	4 large carrots
2 oranges	2 oranges
salt and pepper	salt and pepper
1 tablespoon oil	1 tablespoon oil
sprig of watercress	sprig of watercress

Peel or scrape the carrots according to age, and grate coarsely. Remove the zest from both oranges and squeeze the juice from one orange. Beat in the orange zest, salt and pepper to taste and the oil. Pour the dressing over the grated carrot and chill, covered, in the refrigerator. Meanwhile, peel and divide the other orange into segments. Serve the carrot salad decorated with the fresh orange segments and garnish with a sprig of watercress.

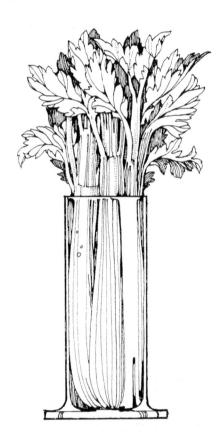

Crisp celery salad

Imperial/Metric	American
1 large head celery	1 large head celery
8 oz./225 g. cooked green peas	½ lb. cooked green peas
6 spring onions, chopped	6 scallions, chopped
dressing:	dressing:
½ teaspoon salt	½ teaspoon salt
¼ teaspoon pepper	¼ teaspoon pepper
1 teaspoon prepared mustard	1 teaspoon prepared mustard
finely grated zest and juice of 1 lime or lemon	finely grated rind and juice of 1 lime or lemon
5 tablespoons oil	6 tablespoons oil
sprig of watercress to garnish	sprig of watercress to garnish

Trim any damaged leaves off the celery, and use for stew or soup. Slice the rest of the celery obliquely into 1 inch/2 cm. lengths. To make the dressing, mix together the salt, pepper, mustard, lime zest and juice. Beat in the oil gradually. Use to toss the vegetables and pile up in a salad bowl. Garnish with a sprig of watercress.

Creamy vegetable casserole

Imperial/Metric
8 oz./225 g. French beans
8 oz./225 g. button onions
12 oz./350 g. corn kernels
2 oz./50 g. butter
3 tablespoons flour
6 tablespoons milk
6 tablespoons single cream
$\frac{1}{4}$ pint/1$\frac{1}{2}$ dl. dry white wine
$\frac{1}{2}$ teaspoon dill weed
$\frac{1}{2}$ teaspoon salt
pinch pepper
$\frac{1}{2}$ teaspoon prepared
  mustard
$\frac{1}{2}$ teaspoon Worcestershire
  sauce
4 oz./125 g. cheese, grated

American
$\frac{1}{2}$ lb. green beans
$\frac{1}{2}$ lb. button onions
$\frac{3}{4}$ lb. corn kernels
$\frac{1}{4}$ cup butter
scant $\frac{1}{4}$ cup all purpose
  flour
$\frac{1}{2}$ cup milk
$\frac{1}{2}$ cup coffee cream
generous $\frac{1}{2}$ cup dry white
  wine
$\frac{1}{2}$ teaspoon dill weed
$\frac{1}{2}$ teaspoon salt
dash pepper
$\frac{1}{2}$ teaspoon prepared
  mustard
$\frac{1}{2}$ teaspoon Worcestershire
  sauce
1 cup grated cheese

Cut the beans into 2 inch/4 cm. lengths and cook with the onions and corn in a little boiling salted water until tender. In a clean pan, melt the butter, stir in the flour. Gradually add milk, cream, wine, herbs and seasonings and bring to the boil, stirring constantly. Add the drained vegetables and turn into an overproof dish. Sprinkle with the cheese and bake in a moderate oven (350°F, 180°C, Gas Mark 4) for about 20 minutes.

Swiss corn salad with tomato petals

Imperial/Metric
3 tomatoes
4 tablespoons French
  dressing
1 large lettuce
4 oz./125 g. cooked
  silverside or tongue
4 oz./125 g. Gruyère cheese
large bunch corn salad

American
3 tomatoes
4 tablespoons Italian
  dressing
1 large lettuce
$\frac{1}{4}$ lb. corned beef
$\frac{1}{4}$ lb. Swiss cheese
large bunch corn salad

Halve the tomatoes, remove seeds and most of the flesh, divide each half into four. Press the flesh and seeds through a sieve and combine the tomato pulp with the dressing. Arrange beds of lettuce leaves in 4 individual salad dishes. Cut the meat and cheese into matchstick lengths. Toss the meat in the tomato dressing. Arrange sprigs of corn salad on the lettuce, divide the meat between the four dishes and top with the cheese sticks. Arrange tomato 'petals' decoratively around the salad.

 # Cucumber sauté

Imperial/Metric
2 medium cucumbers
8 oz./225 g. cooked new
  potatoes
1½ oz./40 g. flour
salt and pepper
2 oz./50 g. butter
1 tablespoon chopped
  parsley
lemon slices

American
2 long cucumbers
½ lb. cooked new potatoes
⅓ cup all-purpose flour
salt and pepper
¼ cup butter
1 tablespoon chopped
  parsley
lemon slices

Peel and cut the cucumbers into ½ inch/ 1 cm. cubes. Cube the potatoes. Season the flour with salt and pepper. Toss the diced potato and cucumber in the seasoned flour. Fry the vegetables in the melted butter until nicely browned, about 15 minutes. Add the chopped parsley. Arrange in a hot serving dish and garnish with the lemon slices.

 # Salade aux chapons

Imperial/Metric
2 large slices stale white
  bread, trimmed
oil for frying
1 clove garlic
4 tablespoons French
  dressing
1 lettuce
½ cucumber
4 spring onions
1 tablespoon chopped
  parsley

American
2 large slices stale white
  bread, trimmed
oil for frying
1 clove garlic
4 tablespoons Italian
  dressing
1 lettuce
½ cucumber
4 scallions
1 tablespoon chopped
  parsley

Cut the bread into very small dice and fry golden brown all over in hot oil. Drain well and cool. Rub the salad bowl with the cut clove of garlic, or crush it and marinate in the salad dressing for at least 2 hours. Shred the lettuce, slice the cucumber and spring onions. Toss together the lettuce, cucumber, onion, parsley and chapons in the dressing and serve immediately.

Cucumber in curd cheese salad

Imperial/Metric
1 large cucumber
salt and pepper
4 oz./125 g. curd cheese
1 tablespoon lemon juice
1 clove garlic, crushed
1 tablespoon chopped
  chives

American
1 long cucumber
salt and pepper
1 cup farmer cheese
1 tablespoon lemon juice
1 clove garlic, crushed
1 tablespoon chopped
  chives

Peel and dice the cucumber. Sprinkle with salt and leave to stand for 1 hour. Rinse in a colander to remove the salt and bitter juices. Beat the cheese with the lemon juice, garlic, pepper to taste and the chives. Fold in the cucumber and chill for 20 minutes before serving.

Summer avocado salad

Imperial/Metric
8 oz./225 g. long grain rice
5 fl. oz./1½ dl. soured
  cream
3 fl. oz./1 dl. French
  dressing
1 teaspoon castor sugar
good pinch ground nutmeg
4 small tomatoes
4 oz./125 g. diced ham
4 oz./125 g. diced cheese
2 avocados
1 tablespoon lemon juice
sprig of parsley

American
½ lb. long grain rice
generous ½ cup
  commercially soured
  cream
scant ½ cup Italian dressing
1 teaspoon granulated
  sugar
good dash nutmeg
⅔ cup diced ham
⅔ cup diced cheese
4 small tomatoes
2 avocados
1 tablespoon lemon juice
sprig of parsley

Cook the rice in plenty of boiling salted water until just tender. Turn into a colander and run fresh boiling water through it. Combine the soured cream, sugar, French dressing and nutmeg to taste. Toss the well drained rice in this dressing while still warm enough to absorb it slightly. Dice the tomatoes, discarding the seeds, and fold into the rice with the ham and cheese. Peel the avocados, cut in half. Remove stones and dice one avocado, cut the other into eight slices lengthways. Toss in the lemon juice, add the diced avocado to the salad, turn into a bowl and decorate with avocado slices and parsley.

Sunburst artichokes

Imperial/Metric
4 globe artichokes
½ pint/3 dl. mayonnaise
1 tablespoon prepared
  mustard
1 tablespoon lemon juice
salt and pepper
4 hard boiled eggs
chopped parsley

American
4 globe artichokes
1¼ cups mayonnaise
1 tablespoon prepared
  mustard
1 tablespoon lemon juice
salt and pepper
4 hard cooked eggs
chopped parsley.

Plunge the artichokes into boiling salted water and boil gently for 30 minutes.
Drain, trim off the points of the leaves and the stalk from the bottom. Chill. Mix the mayonnaise, mustard, lemon juice and salt and pepper to taste. Slice each hard boiled egg into 8 wedges. Pull out the centre leaves and 'choke' from each artichoke and spoon some of the mayonnaise mixture into the centres. Arrange 8 egg wedges around each artichoke. Top with remaining mayonnaise and chopped parsley.

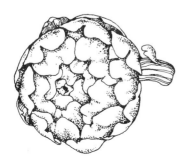

Sweets

The wide choice of seasonal fruits makes it much easier to present the family with mouthwatering desserts such as Greengage strudel and Raspberry cracker meringue; not necessarily expensive but so different from the filling winter fare of pies and puddings.

Greengage strudel

Imperial/Metric
2 lb./1 kg. greengages
3 oz./75 g. ground almonds
1½ oz./40 g. castor sugar
pastry:
12 oz./350 g. flour
pinch of salt
2 tablespoons castor sugar
4 oz./125 g. butter
scant 2 tablespoons water
little milk for brushing

American
2 lb. greengage plums
⅔ cup ground almonds
3 tablespoons granulated sugar
pastry:
3 cups all purpose flour
dash of salt
2 tablespoons granulated sugar
½ cup butter
scant 2 tablespoons water
little milk for brushing

Halve the greengages and remove the stones. Mix together the ground almonds and sugar and sprinkle over the fruit. To make the pastry, sieve the flour with the salt and stir in the sugar. Rub in the butter and add just enough water to make a firm paste. Chill for 30 minutes then roll out thinly into a rectangle. Cover the centre with the fruit, fold in the sides, dampen and press firmly to make a roll. Seal the ends, turn over and place on a buttered baking sheet. Brush with milk and bake in a moderate oven (350°F, 180°C, Gas Mark 4) for 35-40 minutes, until golden brown. Serve warm with cream.

Plum flan with raisin sauce

Imperial/Metric	American
3 oz./75 g. butter	6 tablespoons butter
3 oz./75 g. castor sugar	6 tablespoons granulated sugar
2 eggs	2 eggs
$\frac{1}{2}$ teaspoon vanilla essence	$\frac{1}{2}$ teaspoon vanilla extract
3 oz./75 g. flour	$\frac{3}{4}$ cup all purpose flour
2 oz./50 g. seedless raisins	$\frac{1}{3}$ cup seedless raisins
2 tablespoons rum	2 tablespoons rum
4-5 large yellow or red plums	4-5 large yellow or red plums
4 tablespoons apricot jam	4 tablespoons apricot jam
glacé cherries	candied cherries

Cream the butter and sugar until light and fluffy and gradually beat in the eggs and vanilla essence. Fold in the flour and place the mixture in an 8 inch/20 cm. flan tin. Bake in a moderately hot oven (375°F, 190°C, Gas Mark 5) for 25-30 minutes. Cool on a wire rack. Meanwhile, soak the raisins in the rum. Halve and stone the plums. Heat the jam and sieve it. Mix with the raisins and rum. Place the plums, cut side down, in the flan case, pour over the raisin mixture and decorate with glacé cherries.

Black cherry clafouti

Imperial/Metric	American
2 lb./1 kg. black cherries	2 lb. bing cherries
4 eggs	4 eggs
5 oz./150 g. castor sugar	⅔ cup granulated sugar
2 tablespoons flour	2 tablespoons flour
1 teaspoon vanilla essence	1 teaspoon vanilla extract
2 tablespoons rum	2 tablespoons rum
3 fl. oz./1 dl. milk	scant ½ cup milk
2 tablespoons double cream	2 tablespoons whipping cream

Stone the cherries and place in a buttered shallow ovenproof flan dish. Beat the eggs, sugar and flour together until foamy, then gradually beat in the vanilla essence, rum, milk and cream until the mixture is like a thin pancake batter. Pour over the cherries and bake in a moderately hot oven (375°F, 190°C, Gas Mark 5) for 40 minutes. Serve warm.

Fresh fruit melon compôte

Imperial/Metric	American
¼ pint/1½ dl. grape juice	½ cup grape juice
2 oz./50 g. orange marmalade	¼ cup orange marmalade
2 tablespoons sweet white wine	2 tablespoons sweet white wine
1 large honeydew melon	1 large honeydew melon
½ cantaloupe	½ cantaloupe
4 oz./125 g. green grapes	1 cup green grapes
8 oz./225 g. strawberries	½ lb. strawberries

Combine the grape juice, orange marmalade and sweet white wine. Cut the top off the honeydew melon and remove the seeds. Scoop out the pulp with a melon ball cutter. Dice the pulp from the cantaloupe. Peel and remove the seeds from the grapes. Slice the strawberries in half. Mix the prepared fruits with the grape juice liquid. Spoon into the honeydew melon shell. Chill thoroughly before serving.

Cider and sultana sponge pudding

Imperial/Metric	American
topping:	topping:
¼ pint/1½ dl. medium sweet cider	generous ½ cup cider
4 oz./125 g. sultanas	1 cup seedless white raisins
1 oz./25 g. butter	2 tablespoons butter
2 tablespoons golden syrup	2 tablespoons light corn syrup
sponge:	sponge:
2 oz./50 g. butter	¼ cup butter
4 oz./125 g. castor sugar	½ cup granulated sugar
1 egg	1 egg
6 oz./175 g. plain flour	1½ cups all purpose flour
2 rounded teaspoons baking powder	2 rounded teaspoons baking powder
pinch of salt	dash of salt
cider sauce:	cider sauce:
½ pint/3 dl. medium sweet cider	1¼ cups cider
1 tablespoon golden syrup	1 tablespoon light corn syrup
2 teaspoons cornflour	2 teaspoons cornstarch

First make the topping. Pour the cider over the sultanas, leave to soak overnight, then drain and reserve liquid. Melt the butter and syrup in a small pan and heat until it begins to turn a caramel colour. Pour at once into a greased 7 inch/17.5 cm. cake tin and arrange the soaked sultanas evenly on top. To make the sponge, cream the butter and sugar and gradually beat in the egg. Sieve the flour with the baking powder and salt and fold in with the reserved liquid. If necessary add further cider to give a soft dropping consistency. Pour into the cake tin without disturbing the topping and leave a hollow in the centre. Bake in the centre of a moderate oven (350°F, 180°C, Gas Mark 4) for 50-55 minutes. Turn out at once on a heated dish. Meanwhile, make the sauce. Heat most of the cider with the syrup in a pan. Moisten the cornflour with the remaining cider, add to the pan and bring to the boil, stirring constantly. Simmer for 3 minutes and hand separately with the pudding. Serves 8.

Rhubarb and orange fool with cinnamon fingers

Imperial/Metric
1 orange
1 lb./450 g. rhubarb,
    trimmed
3 oz./75 g. sugar
¼ pint/1½ dl. custard
¼ pint/1½ dl. double cream,
    whipped
cinnamon fingers:
2 slices stale white bread
1½ oz./40 g. butter
1 oz./25 g. castor sugar
½ teaspoon ground
    cinnamon

American
1 orange
1 lb. rhubarb, trimmed
6 tablespoons sugar
generous ½ cup vanilla
    sauce
generous ½ cup whipping
    cream
cinnamon fingers:
2 slices stale white bread
3 tablespoons butter
2 tablespoons granulated
    sugar
½ teaspoon ground
    cinnamon

Grate the zest from the orange and squeeze the juice. Cut the rhubarb into short lengths and cook gently with the orange juice and zest, the sugar and just sufficient water to cover. Cool, and sieve or liquidise in a blender. Stir in the custard, then the cream and pour into a glass serving dish. Chill. To make the fingers, cut the bread into 1 inch/2 cm. lengths. Melt the butter and use to fry the bread. Combine the sugar and cinnamon and sprinkle over the bread fingers when they are golden brown on both sides. Turn until well coated and crisp. Serve warm with the chilled fruit fool.

Strawberry cream flans

Imperial/Metric
2 eggs, separated
2 egg yolks
4 oz./125 g. icing sugar
9 oz./250 g. self-raising
    flour
4 oz./125 g. butter, melted
1 lb./450 g. strawberries,
    halved
pastry cream:
4 egg yolks
2 oz./50 g. flour
4 oz./125 g. castor sugar
1 pint/generous ½ litre
    milk
2 oz./50 g. butter
½ teaspoon vanilla essence

American
2 eggs, separated
2 egg yolks
1 cup sifted confectioners
    sugar
2¼ cups all purpose flour
2½ teaspoons baking
    powder
½ cup butter, melted
1 lb. strawberries,
    halved
pastry cream:
4 egg yolks
½ cup all purpose flour
½ cup granulated sugar
2½ cups milk
¼ cup butter
½ teaspoon vanilla extract

Beat the 4 egg yolks with the sugar until pale and thick. Fold in the flour and the melted butter. Beat the egg whites stiffly and fold into the mixture. Pour into a greased 10 inch/30 cm. fluted flan tin and bake in a moderate oven (350°F, 180°C, Gas Mark 4) for 35-45 minutes. Turn out on a wire rack to cool. To make the pastry cream, beat together the egg yolks, flour and sugar. Heat the milk to boiling point, pour over the mixture and beat well. Return to the saucepan and bring to the boil, stirring constantly, until the mixture is smooth and thickened. Remove from the heat and beat in the butter and vanilla essence. Cool. Split the cake in half and place each half on a serving plate. Press down the soft inside with a metal spoon, fill each half with cream and top with the halved strawberries. Makes 2 flans.

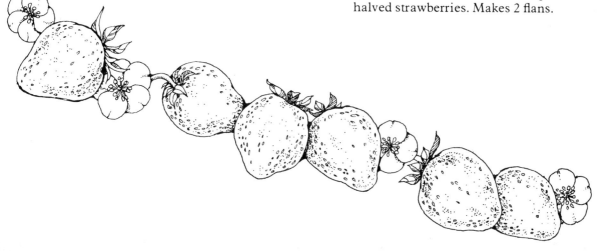

Plum fritters

Imperial/Metric
1½ lb./¾ kg. large fairly
  ripe plums
2 oz./50 g. roughly
  chopped hazelnuts
1 oz./25 g. castor sugar
batter:
7 oz./200 g. plain flour
1 oz./25 g. castor sugar
6 fl. oz./175 ml. milk
2 tablespoons brandy
1 tablespoon oil
3 eggs, separated
oil for frying
castor sugar to sprinkle

American
1½ lb. large fairly ripe
  prune-plums
½ cup coarsely chopped
  hazelnuts
2 tablespoons granulated
  sugar
batter:
1¾ cups all-purpose flour
2 tablespoons granulated
  sugar
¾ cup milk
2 tablespoons brandy
1 tablespoon oil
3 eggs, separated
oil for frying
granulated sugar to
  sprinkle

First make the batter. Sieve the flour into a bowl and stir in the sugar. Gradually beat in the milk, then the brandy, corn oil and finally the egg yolks. Allow to stand in a cool place while you prepare the plums. Choose plums which are just ripe enough to slit open at one side and extract the stone. Mix together the nuts and sugar and use to fill the cavity in each plum, pressing together again into shape. Beat the egg whites until stiff and fold into the batter. Coat each filled plum with the batter and fry in deep hot oil until rich golden brown. Drain and sprinkle liberally with castor sugar. Serve with Red wine sauce.

Red wine sauce

Imperial/Metric
6 fl. oz./175 ml. red wine
6 fl. oz./175 ml. red fruit
  juice or orange juice
2 oz./50 g. sugar
pinch ground cinnamon
1 clove
1 teaspoon cornflour

American
¾ cup red wine
¾ cup red fruit juice or
  orange juice
¼ cup granulated sugar
dash ground cinnamon
1 clove
1 teaspoon cornstarch

Place the wine in a saucepan with the fruit juice, sugar, cinnamon and clove. Bring to boiling point. Moisten the cornflour with a little cold water, add to the pan and bring to the boil again, stirring constantly, until the sauce is thickened and clear. Remove the clove.

Cream puffs with raspberry syrup

Imperial/Metric
2½ oz./65 g. plain flour
pinch of salt
¼ pint/1½ dl. water
2 oz./50 g. butter
2 eggs
¼ pint/1½ dl. double cream
sugar to taste
1 tablespoon sherry
sauce:
8 oz./225 g. raspberries,
  sieved
4 oz./125 g. castor sugar

American
⅔ cup all purpose flour
dash of salt
generous ½ cup water
¼ cup butter
2 eggs
generous ½ cup whipping
  cream
sugar to taste
1 tablespoon sherry
sauce:
½ lb. raspberries,
  sieved
½ cup granulated sugar

First make the puffs. Sieve the flour and salt together. Put the water and butter into a saucepan and bring slowly to the boil. Remove from the heat and beat in the flour to form a ball which leaves the sides of the pan clean. Cool mixture to blood heat, then beat in the eggs, one at a time. Using a ½ inch/1 cm. tube and large piping bag, force about 30 balls of paste, about the size of a walnut, on to wetted baking sheets. Bake in a moderately hot oven (375°F, 190°C, Gas Mark 5) for about 20 minutes, until crisp and pale golden brown. Cool on a wire rack. Whip the cream and sweeten to taste. Stir in the sherry and place in a piping bag with a small nozzle. Make a hole in the base of each puff and pipe in the flavoured cream. Meanwhile, mix together the raspberry purée and castor sugar. Heat slightly to dissolve the sugar. Pile the cream puffs in a glass serving dish and pour over the raspberry sauce.

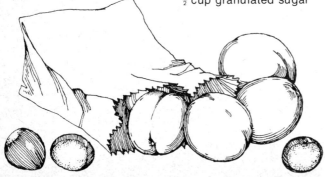

Vicarage trifle

Imperial/Metric
2 large cooking apples
2 oz./50 g. sugar
½ pint/3 dl. thick
 sweetened custard
½ pint/3 dl. double cream
1 red-skinned dessert apple
1 tablespoon lemon juice
2 tablespoons breadcrumbs
 browned in butter
2 tablespoons demerara
 sugar
angelica

American
2 large baking apples
¼ cup sugar
1¼ cups thick vanilla sauce
1¼ cups whipping cream
1 red-skinned eating apple
1 tablespoon lemon juice
3 tablespoons bread
 crumbs browned in
 butter
3 tablespoons brown sugar
angelica

Peel, core and slice the cooking apples, cook with a little water and the sugar until reduced to a purée. Whisk in the custard until smooth. Cool. Half-whip the cream and fold into the apple custard, reserving about one third for the decoration. Pour the apple mixture into a glass serving dish and chill. Core and slice the dessert apple without peeling and toss in the lemon juice to prevent discolouration. Whip the remaining cream until stiff. Toss the buttered crumbs and demerara sugar together and spread over the surface of the apple mixture. Surround the edge of the dish with apple slices, chop the remaining apple and sprinkle over the centre and decorate with rosettes of whipped cream and angelica 'diamonds'.

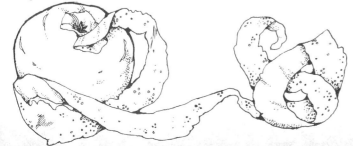

Avocado fruit cocktails

Imperial/Metric
8 oz./225 g. sugar
½ pint/3 dl. water
2 large yellow-fleshed
  peaches
2 medium avocados
4 oz./125 g. grapes
4 oz./125 g. strawberries
2 tablespoons lemon juice
4 tablespoons clear honey

American
1 cup sugar
1¼ cups water
2 large yellow-fleshed
  peaches
2 medium avocados
¼ lb. grapes
¼ lb. strawberries
2 tablespoons lemon juice
4 tablespoons clear honey

Dissolve the sugar in the water over gentle heat then boil for 2 minutes. Pour boiling water over the peaches to loosen the skins and remove them. Halve, remove the stones and slice the peaches into the hot sugar syrup. Chill. Peel the avocados, remove the stones and slice the flesh thinly. Halve and deseed the grapes. Place a few peach slices in the bases of 4 stemmed glasses. Mix together the remaining fruits, pile up decoratively in the glasses and spoon over a little syrup from the peaches. Mix together the lemon juice and honey and warm until well blended. Spoon over the cocktails and serve with small almond biscuits.

 # Melon balls in wine

Imperial/Metric
1 tablespoon mint leaves
1 teaspoon finely grated
  lime zest
2 oz./50 g. sugar
¼ teaspoon salt
8 fl. oz./2½ dl. white wine
2 fl. oz./50 ml. lime juice
1 lb./450 g. mixed melon
  balls (cantaloupe,
  watermelon, honeydew)

American
1 tablespoon mint leaves
1 teaspoon finely grated
  lime rind
¼ cup granulated sugar
¼ teaspoon salt
1 cup white wine
¼ cup lime juice
1 lb. mixed melon balls
  (cantaloupe, watermelon,
  honeydew)

Crush the mint leaves with the lime zest, sugar and salt. Add the wine and lime juice and stir to dissolve the sugar and salt. Allow to stand for 15 minutes. Strain the syrup over the melon balls in a glass serving dish and chill for at least 30 minutes.

 # Cherry bough cake

Imperial/Metric
1 lb./450 g. red cherries
4 oz./125 g. sugar
3 oz./75 g. butter
2 oz./50 g. castor sugar
2 oz./50 g. soft brown
  sugar
1 egg
7 oz./200 g. self-raising
  flour
1 teaspoon baking powder
½ teaspoon salt
6 fl. oz./175 ml. milk

American
1 lb. red cherries
½ cup sugar
⅓ cup butter
¼ cup granulated sugar
¼ cup brown sugar
1 egg
1¾ cups all-purpose flour
2½ teaspoons baking
  powder
½ teaspoon salt
¾ cup milk

Stone and chop the cherries. Mix with 4 oz./125 g. white sugar and let stand 15 minutes. Cream the butter with the castor and brown sugars. Beat in the egg. Sieve the flour with the baking powder and salt. Fold into the creamed mixture alternately with the milk. Drain the chopped cherries, reserving the liquid. Fold the drained cherries into the batter. Turn into a greased and floured 9 inch/23 cm. cake tin. Bake in a moderate oven (350°F, 180°C, Gas Mark 4) for 30-35 minutes. Serve warm with Cherry sauce. Serves 8.

 # Cherry sauce

Imperial/Metric
2 tablespoons cornflour
2 tablespoons castor sugar
pinch of salt
½ pint/3 dl. cherry juice
3 drops almond essence

American
2 tablespoons cornstarch
2 tablespoons granulated
  sugar
dash of salt
1¼ cups cherry juice
3 drops almond extract

Mix the cornflour, sugar and salt with a little water to make a smooth paste. Add enough water to the reserved cherry juice to make ½ pint/3 dl. cherry liquid. Stir the cornflour paste into the cherry liquid and cook over low heat until thickened. Stir in the almond essence.

Banana and strawberry cream

Imperial/Metric	American
4 large ripe bananas	4 large ripe bananas
4 oz./125 g. castor sugar	$\frac{1}{2}$ cup granulated sugar
juice of $\frac{1}{2}$ lemon	juice of $\frac{1}{2}$ lemon
$\frac{1}{4}$ pint/1$\frac{1}{2}$ dl. double cream	generous $\frac{1}{2}$ cup whipping cream
$\frac{1}{4}$ pint/1$\frac{1}{2}$ dl. single cream	generous $\frac{1}{2}$ cup coffee cream
8 oz./225 g. strawberries, hulled	$\frac{1}{2}$ lb. strawberries, hulled
vanilla ice cream	vanilla ice cream
toasted almonds	toasted almonds

Mash the bananas with the sugar and lemon juice. Whip the two creams together. Fold in the banana purée, then the whole strawberries. Serve over scoops of vanilla ice cream and top with toasted almonds.

 # Peach and strawberry flambé

Imperial/Metric	American
4 fresh peaches	4 fresh peaches
1 pint/generous $\frac{1}{2}$ litre water	2$\frac{1}{2}$ cups water
4 oz./125 g. sugar	$\frac{1}{2}$ cup granulated sugar
1 long strip lemon rind	1 long strip lemon rind
$\frac{1}{4}$ stick cinnamon	$\frac{1}{4}$ stick cinnamon
8 oz./225 g. fresh strawberries	$\frac{1}{2}$ lb. fresh strawberries
1 teaspoon grated orange zest	1 teaspoon grated orange rind
2 fl. oz./50 ml. brandy	$\frac{1}{4}$ cup brandy

Place the unpeeled peaches in a saucepan. Combine the water and sugar and pour over the peaches. Add the lemon rind and cinnamon stick. Bring to the boil and simmer 15 minutes. Take out the peaches, skin, cut in half and remove the stones. Place the peach halves, cut side down, in a chafing dish. Crush the strawberries, add the orange zest and $\frac{1}{4}$ pint/1$\frac{1}{2}$ dl./$\frac{1}{2}$ cup of peach syrup. Pour over the peaches and heat gently. Warm the brandy, pour into the chafing dish and light with a match. Serve immediately with cream or over vanilla ice cream.

 # Raspberry cracker meringue

Imperial/Metric	American
8 cream crackers	22 soda crackers
3 egg whites	3 egg whites
6 oz./175 g. castor sugar	$\frac{3}{4}$ cup granulated sugar
$\frac{1}{2}$ teaspoon baking powder	$\frac{1}{2}$ teaspoon baking powder
2 oz./50 g. chopped walnuts	$\frac{1}{2}$ cup chopped walnuts
$\frac{1}{4}$ pint/1$\frac{1}{2}$ dl. double cream	$\frac{1}{2}$ cup whipping cream
2 oz./50 g. castor sugar	$\frac{1}{4}$ cup granulated sugar
$\frac{1}{2}$ teaspoon vanilla essence	$\frac{1}{2}$ teaspoon vanilla extract
8 oz./225 g. fresh raspberries	$\frac{1}{2}$ lb. fresh raspberries

Place the cream crackers in a polythene bag and crush with a rolling pin. Whisk the egg whites until frothy. Gradually whisk in the 6 oz./175 g. sugar and the baking powder. Continue whisking until very stiff peaks form. Fold in the cracker crumbs and chopped walnuts. Pile into a lightly greased 10 inch/25 cm. flan dish. Bake in a moderate oven (350°F, 180°C, Gas Mark 4) for 30-35 minutes. Let cool. Whisk the cream lightly, gradually add one teaspoon of the sugar and the vanilla essence. Spoon the remaining sugar over the fresh raspberries. Fold the raspberries into the whipped cream. Spoon over the cooled meringue. Refrigerate until serving time. Serves 8.

Chilled pineapple poll

Imperial/Metric
15 oz./425 g. can pine-
  apple slices
1 pineapple jelly
15½ oz./430 g. can creamed
  rice
¼ pint/1½ dl. double cream
angelica

American
15 oz. can pineapple
  slices
1 package pineapple
  flavored gelatin
15½ oz. can creamed rice
  pudding
generous ½ cup whipping
  cream
angelica

Strain the syrup from the pineapple into
a medium sized saucepan. Reserve 4
pineapple rings and chop the remainder.
Break up the jelly, add to the syrup and
heat gently to dissolve. Stir in the creamed
rice and chopped pineapple. Divide the
mixture between 4 individual dishes.
Leave in a cool place until set. Whisk the
cream until stiff and place in a piping
bag. Put a slice of pineapple on top of
each dessert. Pipe with large rosettes of
cream and decorate with angelica 'leaves'.
Serve chilled.

69

Jams and preserves

Become noted for your home-made preserves, always a talking point round the table when the recipes are as unusual as these.

Amber marrow jam

Imperial/Metric
1 large marrow
sugar
2 oranges
2 lemons
2 oz./50 g. stem ginger, chopped
2 tablespoons ginger syrup
pinch ground ginger

American
1 large squash
granulated sugar
2 oranges
2 lemons
¼ cup preserved ginger, chopped
2 tablespoons ginger syrup
dash ground ginger

Peel the marrow, remove the pith and seeds, dice finely and weigh. To 3lb./1¼ kg. marrow allow an equal weight of sugar. Put alternate layers of diced marrow and sugar in a large bowl, ending with a layer of sugar. Cover and leave to stand overnight. Grate the zest from the oranges and lemons and squeeze the juice. Transfer the contents of the bowl to a preserving pan and bring to the boil, stirring. Add the fruit zests and juices, the chopped ginger and syrup and the ground ginger. Cook steadily until the marrow becomes a pulp. Test for setting by placing a drop on a saucer. If tilting the saucer causes the jam to wrinkle it is done. Pour into warm dry pots, seal and label. Makes about 4½ lb./2 kg.

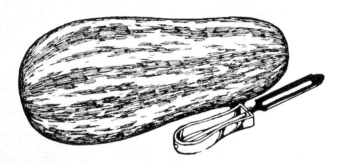

Tomato marmalade

Imperial/metric
1 lb./450 g. tomatoes
grated zest and juice of
  1 large sweet orange
juice of 1 lemon
1 lb./450 g. granulated
  sugar

American
1 lb. tomatoes
grated rind and juice of
  1 large sweet orange
juice of 1 lemon
2 cups sugar

Skin and chop the tomatoes and place in a wide pan with the grated zest and citrus juices. Simmer over a moderate heat, stirring occasionally, until the mixture is soft and pulpy. (This will take about 15 minutes.) Add the sugar and stir until it has completely dissolved. Bring to the boil and keep at a full, rolling boil until the setting point is reached. Test as for jam. Allow to cool slightly. Makes about 2 lb./1 kg.

Canteloupe melon jam

Imperial/Metric
1 large cantaloupe melon
2 lb./scant 1 kg. sugar
1 large lemon
$\frac{1}{2}$ teaspoon ground ginger

American
1 large cantaloupe melon
4 cups sugar
1 large lemon
$\frac{1}{2}$ teaspoon ground ginger

Peel the zest from the lemon thinly, and chop into fine shreds. Peel the melon, cut half and remove pips, straining off and reserving juice. Cut flesh into small cubes, add to the juice with the shredded lemon zest, sugar and ground ginger, and allow to stand overnight. Stir well, add the squeezed lemon juice and bring to the boil. Cook rapidly until quite clear, about 20 minutes. Pour into clean warm jars and seal.

Elegant peach preserve

Imperial/Metric
8 large peaches
2 large oranges
4 oz./100 g. Maraschino
  cherries
juice 2 lemons
3 lb./1$\frac{1}{4}$ kg. sugar

American
8 large peaches
2 large oranges
$\frac{1}{2}$ cup Maraschino cherries
juice 2 lemons
6 cups sugar

Halve the peaches, remove stones and roughly dice the flesh. Grate the zest from the oranges, cut them in half and spoon out the flesh. Put the diced peaches, orange zest and flesh, lemon juice and sugar in a preserving pan. Bring to the boil. Add the halved cherries and their juice, and cook rapidly until the preserve sets when tested. Pour into warm clean jars. Allow to stand until cold, stir to distribute the fruit, and seal.

Almond apricot conserve

Imperial/Metric
2 large oranges
3 lb./1$\frac{1}{4}$ kg. apricots
3 lb./1$\frac{1}{4}$ kg. sugar
2 oz./50 g. ground almonds

American
2 large oranges
3 lb. apricots
2 oz. ground almonds
6 cups sugar

Peel the zest from the oranges thinly, cut them in half and spoon out the flesh. Roughly chop the zest. Cover with water, bring to the boil and cook for 4 minutes. Strain off the water, add the softened zest to the halved and stoned apricots. (If large, quarter the apricots.) Put the orange flesh, zest and apricots in a preserving pan and cook gently until the apricots are soft. Add the ground almonds and sugar and bring back to the boil. Cook rapidly until the conserve sets when tested. Pour into warm clean jars and seal.

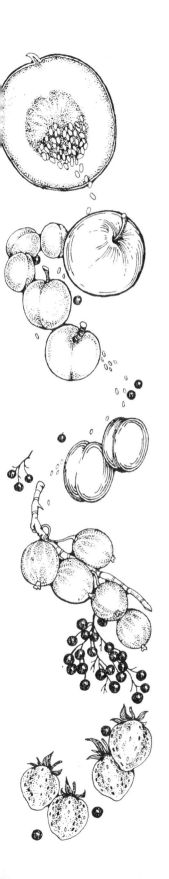

Seasonal home freezing

This is the time of year when you will find your freezer really worth its weight in gold. No longer will you be stuck in the kitchen – even during the school holidays or when you have visitors – on sunny days.

Freeze down the soft fruits in whichever way best suits your particular need, or freeze down some by each of the methods given. You will find the fruits invaluable for quick desserts to serve as they are, or to turn into mousses, soufflés and fruit fools.

Home-made ice cream is not difficult or too expensive to make and many varieties can be made by adding a different fruit purée to the basic ice cream.

Make sure you have a good stock of poultry, which is ideal for summer meals. This will help towards making catering for your family, friends and unexpected visitors during the summer months a great deal easier, and allow you to enjoy the sunshine.

Basic methods of freezing fruit

Fruit is a good 'freezable' and has a storage life averaging 1 year. There are four ways of freezing fruit and the method you choose really depends on the type of fruit you intend to freeze. For example, the soft fruits give the best results when thawed, if they are open frozen. However, there is no reason if you prefer a softer result with some juice, why you should not use the dry sugar or sugar syrup methods.

All fruit for freezing (like any other food) should be in peak condition – neither over-ripe nor under-ripe. It is not worth investing your time, effort, freezer space, and packaging materials in food which is less than perfect. It is better to use any slightly damaged fruit immediately, or cut out the bad parts and purée the remainder.

Dry sugar method: This method is suitable for prepared apples, apricots, plums and greengages, rhubarb intended for cooking, pineapple, melon and citrus fruits, and the soft berry fruits – strawberries, raspberries, blackcurrants, redcurrants and gooseberries.

To prepare soft fruit for dry sugar packing, hull the fruit then carefully wash it in small quantities – this prevents it from becoming crushed – and dry gently with kitchen paper, or allow to drain thoroughly. Halve and stone apricots, plums and greengages; peel, quarter and core apples.

As the name of this method suggests, a layer of the prepared fruit is packed in a container (rigid-based polythene containers are the most suitable) and sprinkled with sugar. Continue to layer the fruit and sugar until the container is full, leaving a small headspace. Seal and label in the usual way. With the soft fruits it is a good idea to place a foil divider halfway up the pack to help support the weight of the top layer and prevent the fruit underneath from becoming crushed during defrosting.

An alternative method of packing in dry sugar is to place the prepared fruit in a bowl with the sugar and turn the fruit gently with a wooden spoon until it is lightly and evenly coated, then transfer to the containers.

Amounts of sugar to use: Allow approximately 1 lb./450 g./2 cups sugar to 3-5 lb./1½-2½ kg. fruit, depending on its natural sweetness. Use granulated or castor sugar, or icing sugar if a smooth syrup is required. There is bound to be some syrup in the pack when fully

defrosted, but the smaller grain used, the smoother the syrup. It is possible to pack fruit without any sugar if you know you are likely to want unsweetened fruit for certain recipes.

Sugar syrup method: A suitable method for apples, pears, damsons, figs, citrus fruit, grapes, plums, melon, peaches and pineapple.

The choice of syrup strength depends on two factors—one, whether the flavour of the fruit is light and delicate and may be overwhelmed by a heavy sugar syrup and two, whether the fruit is naturally rather sharp and may be improved by being frozen in a heavy syrup. A medium heavy syrup is ideal for most fruits.

Make up the syrup according to kind—see the chart below—and allow it to cool. Prepare the fruit; apples and other fruits which discolour when exposed to the air must be sprinkled with lemon juice, or put into a salt water or ascorbic acid solution ($\frac{1}{4}$ teaspoon ascorbic acid crystals in 4 tablespoons water).

Sugar	Water	Strength (%)
2 oz./50 g./$\frac{1}{4}$ cup	1 pint/6 dl./$2\frac{1}{2}$ cups	very thin (10%)
4 oz./125 g./$\frac{1}{2}$ cup	1 pint/6 dl./$2\frac{1}{2}$ cups	thin (20%)
7 oz./200 g./scant 1 cup	1 pint/6 dl./$2\frac{1}{2}$ cups	medium thin (30%)
11 oz./300 g./scant 1$\frac{1}{2}$ cups	1 pint/6 dl./$2\frac{1}{2}$ cups	medium heavy (40%)
1 lb./450 g./2 cups	1 pint/6 dl./$2\frac{1}{2}$ cups	heavy (50%)
1 lb. 9 oz./700 g./ generous 3 cups	1 pint/6 dl./$2\frac{1}{2}$ cups	very heavy (60%)

Pack the prepared fruit into polythene containers and pour over sufficient chilled syrup just to cover the fruit. Allow a $\frac{1}{2}$ inch/1 cm. headspace, and to prevent the fruit from rising in the syrup, crumple a piece of foil a little larger than the top of the container, and press down lightly on the fruit. You will find that the foil will freeze into the syrup but when the pack has defrosted it can be removed easily. Seal and label in the usual way.

Open freezing method: This method is particularly suitable for the delicate soft berry fruits as it produces the most satisfactory result when the fruit has defrosted. It ensures the fastest freezing possible, by exposing all surfaces of the fruit to cold air. When packed closely, the centre fruits would take much longer to freeze down.

The fruit must first be washed if necessary, a small quantity at a time to prevent squashing and bruising, and then thoroughly dried on kitchen paper. Hull the fruit *after* it has been washed to avoid pockets of water. Arrange the fruit, spaced well apart, on clean baking sheets (making sure that they can be easily accommodated in the freezer) and place in the freezer until hard—it is a good idea to use the fast

freeze switch for this operation – about 1-2 hours. Remove the baking sheets from the freezer and quickly pack the frozen fruit into shallow polythene containers, or polythene bags with foil dividers to prevent the lower layers of fruit being squashed. Seal and label in the usual way. With this method it is not necessary to leave a headspace in the container as the fruit is already frozen when it is packed.

These soft fruits are nicest and have a slightly firmer texture if they are served when they are still slightly chilled.

Purée method: Any fruit which can be stewed (either on top of the cooker or in the oven) and made into a purée by sieving or blending can be packed in this form. The purée can be sweetened to taste or frozen unsweetened. Soft fruits can be puréed without cooking. This method is excellent for using *slightly* damaged fruit as the bruised parts can be discarded.

When cooking fruit for a purée, use the minimum amount of water – about 4 tablespoons to each 1 lb./450 g. prepared fruit. Cool the purée quickly, then pack into containers leaving a $\frac{1}{2}$ inch/1 cm. headspace. Seal and label in the usual way remembering to state on the label whether the purée has had sugar added or has been frozen unsweetened. Purées of uncooked fruit can be sweetened by adding castor or icing sugar to taste in a blender, or dissolving the sugar in the purée completely while still hot or by adding a small quantity of heavy sugar syrup to the purée.

To freeze fruits that discolour easily: A coloured syrup disguises discolouration. For this reason freeze pears in a syrup tinted pink, apricots and peaches in a syrup tinted yellow.

Fruit purées are ideal for young babies and can also be made into a variety of tempting desserts – fruit fools, mousses, creams, ice creams and sorbets.

Fruit fool: Mix together equal quantities of defrosted fruit purée and cold custard, or half cream and half custard or all cream. (Canned custard is excellent in a fruit fool and makes the preparation even easier.) Add sugar to taste, depending on whether the purée was frozen with or without sugar and the natural sweetness of the fruit. Serve in individual glasses with ratafias, brandy snaps or Florentine biscuits.

Fruit snow: Place $\frac{1}{2}$ pint/3 dl./$1\frac{1}{4}$ cups fruit purée, or a mixture of purées, in a bowl. Fold in 2 stiffly beaten egg whites and sweeten if necessary. Serve in individual dishes.

Soft fruit sorbets: Although cirtus fruit sorbets are more usual, all soft fruits can be used. Here are two alternative methods, the first being suitable for naturally sweet fruits such as strawberries or raspberries, the latter for sharper fruits such as loganberries, redcurrants and blackcurrants.

Redcurrant sorbet

Imperial/Metric
¾ pint/4½ dl. redcurrant purée
1 teaspoon gelatine
2 egg whites

American
scant 2 cups redcurrant purée
1 teaspoon unflavored gelatin
2 egg whites

Heat a little of the fruit purée and add the gelatine. Allow it to dissolve then add the remaining purée and stir well. Turn into a bowl, cover the surface with freezer film and place in the freezer until the mixture has thickened slightly. Remove and fold in the stiffly beaten egg whites. Transfer to a suitable container, seal, label and freeze.

Strawberry sorbet

Imperial/Metric
¾ pint/4½ dl. sweetened strawberry purée
2 tablespoons lemon juice
4 tablespoons orange juice

American
scant 2 cups sweetened strawberry purée
2 tablespoons lemon juice
4 tablespoons orange juice

Blend the purée with the fruit juices and pour into a shallow container. Cover with freezer film and freeze until ice crystals begin to form. Remove from the freezer, beat thoroughly, return to the container and freeze until firm. (The consistency will be more like that of an Italian 'Granita', but is very pleasant.)

Raspberry mousse

Imperial/Metric
1 pint/generous ½ litre raspberry purée
2 oz./50 g. cream cheese
2 tablespoons castor sugar
½ oz./15 g. gelatine
4 tablespoons cold water
¼ pint/1½ dl. double cream
2 egg whites
decoration:
¼ pint/1½ dl. double cream
fresh or frozen raspberries

American
2½ cups raspberry purée
¼ cup cream cheese
3 tablespoons granulated sugar
1 tablespoon unflavored gelatin
⅓ cup cold water
⅔ cup heavy cream
2 egg whites
decoration:
⅔ cup heavy cream
fresh or frozen raspberries

Mix together the raspberry purée, cream cheese and castor sugar. Put the gelatine and water in a small pan and place over low heat until the gelatine has dissolved. Remove from the heat and allow to cool. Gradually add the dissolved gelatine to the raspberry mixture, whisking to combine the ingredients. Leave the mixture aside until it is beginning to set, then fold in the lightly whipped cream and stiffly beaten egg whites. Turn into a large dish or six individual dishes and chill in the refrigerator until firm. Before serving, pipe a decoration of whipped cream and top with the raspberries. Serves 6.
Note: Other fruit purées—strawberry, apricot or blackcurrant—may be used in place of the raspberry purée.

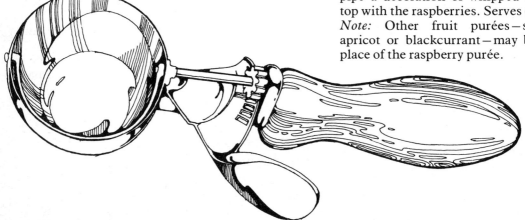

Blackcurrant soufflé

Imperial/Metric
½ oz./15 g. gelatine
3 tablespoons cold water
4 egg yolks
2 oz./50 g. castor sugar
½ pint/3 dl. sweetened
  blackcurrant purée
¼ pint/1½ dl. double cream
4 egg whites
decoration:
chopped toasted almonds
whipped cream

American
1 tablespoon unflavored
  gelatin
3 tablespoons cold water
4 egg yolks
¼ cup granulated sugar
1¼ cups sweetened
  blackcurrant purée
generous ½ cup heavy cream
4 egg whites
decoration:
chopped toasted almonds
whipped cream.

First prepare a 7 inch/18 cm. soufflé dish by tying a band of double thickness greaseproof paper around the outside to come about 2 inches/5 cm. above the top of the dish. Put the gelatine and cold water in a small pan and place over low heat until the gelatine has dissolved. Cool. Place the egg yolks and castor sugar in a bowl and whisk over hot water until the mixture is thick and light in colour. Remove from the heat and continue to whisk the mixture until it is cool. (If using a mixer it is not necessary to whisk over hot water.) Blend in the purée, then stir in the dissolved gelatine. Finally, fold in the lightly whipped cream and stiffly whisked egg whites. Pour into the prepared dish and leave to set in the refrigerator. To serve, carefully remove the band of paper and press chopped almonds into the sides of the soufflé. Decorate with whipped cream.

Loganberry ice cream

Imperial/Metric
½ pint/3 dl. creamy milk
2 eggs, separated
3 oz./75 g. castor sugar
1 vanilla pod
8 fl. oz./2½ dl. loganberry
  purée
¾ pint/4½ dl. double cream

American
1¼ cups creamy milk
2 eggs, separated
6 tablespoons granulated
  sugar
1 vanilla bean
1 cup loganberry purée
scant 2 cups heavy cream

Put the milk, egg yolks, sugar and vanilla pod in a bowl placed over a pan of hot water. Cook over the heat until the custard thickens sufficiently to coat the back of a spoon. Remove from the heat, discard the vanilla pod and leave the custard to cool. When cold, stir in the fruit purée. Fold in the fairly stiffly whipped cream and stiffly beaten egg whites. Place the mixture in a clean bowl, cover lightly with freezer film and place in the freezer until the mixture is partially frozen. Take out and beat the mixture until it is smooth then transfer to a suitable container for freezing. Seal and label.
Note: To make a fruit and nut ice cream, add 4 oz./125 g./¾ cup chopped hazelnuts or almonds.

To prepare fish for freezing

It is only advisable to freeze fish if you are able to obtain it freshly caught. If not, it is better to purchase commercially frozen fish and store it in your freezer.

White fish — cod, halibut, haddock, etc. — can be stored for up to 6 months, but oily fish such as herring, mackerel or salmon, should be kept only for up to 3 months.

Prepare the fish according to kind: small fish can be frozen whole, cleaned and gutted; larger fish in steaks or fillets. Dip the prepared fish in a bowl of iced water, drain thoroughly, open freeze, then wrap with dividers between each portion. If the portions are awkward in shape, mould each one in foil, then pack all together in a polythene container. Seal and label.

To freeze white fish: Remove fins, tail and scrape away the scales. Gut and wash well in cold water. Dip portions of fish in a weak brine solution — 2 oz./50 g./$\frac{1}{4}$ cup salt to 2 pints/generous 1 litre/5 cups water — drain, wrap, label and freeze.

To freeze oily fish: Remove fins, tail, and scrape away the scales. Gut and wash well. Dip portions in an ascorbic acid solution — 2 teaspoons ascorbic acid to 2 pints/generous 1 litre/5 cups water — drain, wrap, label and freeze. With oily fish it is particularly important to ensure that they are adequately wrapped to prevent them drying out and becoming freezer burnt.

Polythene bags are available which are just the right size and shape for large fish, and make it much easier to pack these separately. Whole salmon, or salmon trout, can be wrapped in 'Look' roasting film, sealing the metal edges together down the centre of the back and sealing the ends with twist ties. The whole fish can then be transferred straight from the freezer to the oven, and treated in one of two ways. Either allow to defrost fully, allowing 4-6 hours according to the size of the fish; then

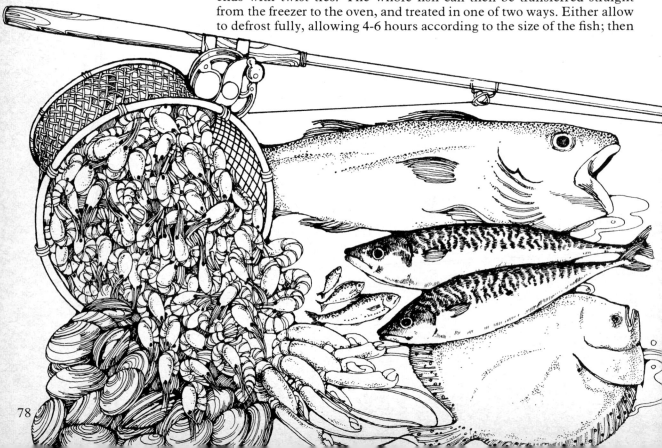

light the oven, and allow the usual length of time for cooking. Or, cook at a very low temperature from the frozen state, adding 1 hour to cooking time for defrosting.

To freeze shellfish: It is only advisable to freeze down shellfish on the same day as it is caught as it is even more perishable than white and oily fish. The most satisfactory results are obtained with freezing prawns and shrimps, but other shellfish can be frozen for 2-3 months.

To freeze prawns and shrimps: Place, raw, in boiling salted water for 3-5 minutes, depending on the size. Cool quickly then shell. Pack in polythene containers, leaving a headspace, or in bags, seal and label. Store for 1 month.

To freeze *potted shrimps*, shell the cooked shrimps and blend with sufficient melted butter to give a good coating. Season with black pepper and a pinch of ground nutmeg. Pack in small containers (empty washed yogurt or cream cartons are ideal) and cover with a layer of clarified butter. Chill and cover the butter with a layer of freezer film, then seal and label.

To freeze lobster and crab: Kill, bring to the boil in salted water allowing 15 minutes per lb./450 g. Drain, open, remove the meat (discarding the uneatable stomach and intestinal cord) and pack in polythene containers or bags. Seal and label.

To freeze oysters: Scrub thoroughly, remove from the shells, dip in salt water and pack in polythene containers with the shell liquid. Seal and label.

To freeze mussels: Prepare in the normal way and freeze in the cooking liquid in polythene containers, leaving a headspace. Use in soups, etc.

Do take care in packing fish for the freezer, otherwise cross contamination of other foods with the fishy odours and flavours will occur. If possible enclose all fish and shellfish packs in a large polythene container or a batching bag.

Freezer jams

Some fruits are suitable for making delicious *uncooked* jams which can be stored in the freezer for at least six months. Compared to the traditional jam-making method, they are extremely easy to prepare and have a natural, sweet, fresh-fruit flavour.

The following fruits (or combination of fruits) are suitable for making freezer jams: blackberries, blackcurrants, loganberries, raspberries, redcurrants, rhubarb and strawberries.

Place the prepared fruit in a bowl. To 2 lb./1 kg. fruit add 3½ lb./ 1¾ kg. castor sugar and 4 tablespoons lemon juice. Stir well and leave to stand until the sugar has dissolved completely. This may take from about 20 minutes to 2 hours, depending on the amount of juice in the fruit. Stir in a scant ½ pint/2½ dl./1 cup commercial pectin and continue to stir until the mixture is beginning to set. Ladle into polythene tumblers, leaving a small headspace, seal and label.

To use the jam, for spreading or as a filling, allow to defrost at room temperature for about 30 minutes. This type of jam never freezes solid and remains viscous at average storage temperature because of the high sugar content.

Dessert sauces

A selection of sweet sauces to serve with ice cream and other chilled desserts is always an asset in the freezer. Store sauces in rigid based polythene tumblers leaving a headspace. To serve hot, defrost and re-heat in a double saucepan or over hot water.

Mocha sauce: Place 8 oz./225 g. plain chocolate in the top of a double boiler, or a bowl placed over a pan of hot water, and heat until melted. Stir in 2 oz./50 g. butter and 6 tablespoons strong black coffee. Mix together until the sauce is smooth and glossy. Cool slightly, then pour into a polythene tumbler. When cold, seal, label and freeze.

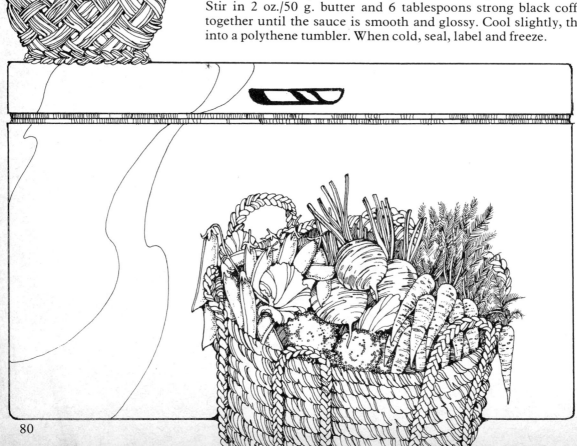

To prepare poultry for freezing

All poultry freezes well and can be frozen whole, in portions or made up into cooked dishes. It is absolutely imperative to ensure that whole, uncooked poultry and smaller portions are completely defrosted before being cooked so that during cooking sufficient heat penetrates to the centre of the poultry killing any harmful bacteria present.

To freeze poultry whole: Clean and wipe the inside with a damp cloth, tie the legs with string and press the wings closely to the body. To prevent the bone ends piercing the wrapping, protect them with several thicknesses of foil or with greaseproof paper secured with a rubber band. Do not pack the giblets inside the cavity of the bird or add any stuffing. Both should be frozen separately. If more convenient prepare stock using the giblets and freeze that in the form of cubes or in a polythene container. The whole bird can be wrapped in freezer foil moulding it closely to the shape of the bird, or placed in a gussetted polythene bag. If storing in a bag, remove as much air as possible before sealing with a twist tie and taping down the corners with freezer tape. Label and freeze.

To freeze halved poultry: Whole poultry does take up a large area of valuable freezer space, therefore you may prefer to freeze it in halves. Place the bird on one side and cut from the neck to the tail end keeping as closely as possible along each side of the backbone. Remove the neck and backbone. Place the bird breast-side down, pull it open and cut along the inside of the breastbone. Either pack the halves together as for whole poultry, separating them with a foil divider, or separately.

If you have a sufficient quantity of poultry livers, turn them into a pâté for freezing. An excellent pâté can be made by frying lightly floured livers and some chopped onion in a little butter. Allow to cool slightly then blend in the liquidiser until smooth. Mix in some dry sherry, double cream and seasoning to taste. Smooth into small polythene containers, seal and label.

To freeze portions: These are a very useful standby in the freezer. The supplier will be able to joint the poultry for you, or you can do it quite easily with a sharp knife and a pair of poultry scissors. Use the carcases and trimmings to make stock for freezing. After jointing wipe the portions with a damp cloth and mould each portion in foil. Pack a convenient number of portions together, in a batching bag or large container then seal and label.

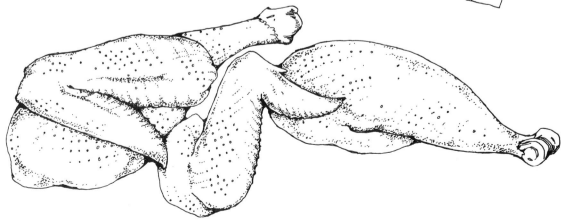

Summer gardening hints

Early Summer

Pinch out the growing tip of cucumbers in frames.

Thin out young shoots on seakale leaving the best one on each plant for a good crown to develop.

Lift early potatoes and thin out spinach seedlings grown earlier.

Leeks and Savoy cabbages can be planted now. Sow more lettuce seeds, and a row of parsley for Winter and Spring use.

In the greenhouse tomatoes should be ripening fast so the fruit must be picked regularly. Remove all side shoots and lower leaves from the plants.

Mid Summer

Make a further sowing of a dwarf early-maturing pea recommended for freezing — Meteor or Kelvedon Wonder.

Sow more salad onions for succession.

If the weather is dry, water runner beans freely and syringe daily with water to help the flowers set. Outdoor tomatoes will also need watering if the weather is dry.

Carefully lift shallots and garlic and lay them in the sun to dry.

As well as freezing herbs for future use, a store of dried herbs is an asset. Tie the herbs in small bundles and suspend, head down, in a cool airy room, but not in strong sunlight.

Late Summer

Continue to water runner beans freely if the weather is dry.

Make a further sowing of lettuce for Autumn use.

Cut marrows while they are young and tender before the outer skin hardens and sets.

Gather French and runner beans regularly before they become tough and stringy and freeze down surplus supplies.

Sow spring cabbage seed in well-worked but firm soil.

Brussels sprouts and other winter greens will benefit if fed with a sprinkling of a compound fertiliser around the plants.

Super Garden Relishes

Sweet and sour mustard beans

Imperial/metric	American
2 lb./1 kg. runner beans	2 lb. green or wax beans
8 oz./225 g. castor sugar	1 cup granulated sugar
3 tablespoons plain flour	3 tablespoons all-purpose flour
3 tablespoons dry mustard	3 tablespoons dry mustard
2 teaspoons celery seed	2 teaspoons celery seed
2 teaspoons ground turmeric	2 teaspoons ground turmeric
$\frac{1}{2}$ pint/3 dl. white vinegar	$1\frac{1}{4}$ cups white vinegar

Slice the beans in 1 inch/2.5 cm. lengths. Cook in boiling salted water until tender. Drain. Mix the remaining ingredients in a saucepan. Cook over low heat for 3 minutes until slightly thickened. Add the beans and cook 5 minutes longer. Pour into hot clean jars. Seal.
Makes $1\frac{1}{2}$ pints/scant 1 litre/4 cups.

Raspberry and currant relish

Imperial/Metric	American
2 lb./1 kg. raspberries	2 lb. raspberries
1 lb./450 g. red currants	1 lb. red currants
$\frac{1}{2}$ pint/3 dl. wine vinegar	$1\frac{1}{4}$ cups wine vinegar
$\frac{1}{2}$ teaspoon salt	$\frac{1}{2}$ teaspoon salt
$\frac{1}{2}$ teaspoon dry mustard	$\frac{1}{2}$ teaspoon dry mustard
$\frac{1}{2}$ teaspoon allspice	$\frac{1}{2}$ teaspoon allspice
sugar	sugar

Stew the fruit gently in the vinegar until it is a pulp. Sieve, pressing through everything except the seeds, back into the pan. Add the salt, mustard and allspice. Simmer gently for 20 minutes, then strain again. Measure the liquid, and add 6 oz./160 g./$\frac{2}{3}$ cup sugar to each pint/ generous $\frac{1}{2}$ litre/$1\frac{1}{4}$ pints liquid. Bring slowly to the boil again, dissolve sugar over moderate heat, then boil rapidly until thick. Pour into warm clean jars and seal.

Granny's red cabbage relish

Imperial/Metric	American
8 oz./225 g. red cabbage, shredded	1 cup red cabbage, shredded
1 tablespoon brown sugar	1 tablespoon brown sugar
$\frac{1}{2}$ teaspoon salt	½ teaspoon salt
3 tablespoons vinegar	3 tablespoons vinegar
$\frac{1}{4}$ teaspoon celery seed	¼ teaspoon celery seed
1 teaspoon dry mustard	1 teaspoon dry mustard

Mix the seasonings well, stir into the vinegar, and add the sugar. Beat with a fork to dissolve the sugar. Pack the shredded cabbage firmly into a polythene container, pour over the vinegar mixture, and seal. Keep in the refrigerator for at least a week before serving. Turn the container over every day.

Spiced conference pears

Imperial/Metric	American
3 lb./$2\frac{1}{4}$ kg. hard pears	3 lb. hard pears
$\frac{1}{2}$ pint/3 dl. vinegar	generous cup vinegar
1 lb. soft brown sugar	1 lb. soft brown sugar
1 in./$2\frac{1}{2}$ cm. stick cinnamon	1 in. stick cinnamon
$\frac{1}{2}$ teaspoon ground cloves	$\frac{1}{2}$ teaspoon ground cloves
$\frac{1}{4}$ teaspoon ground mace	$\frac{1}{4}$ teaspoon ground mace

Make the spiced syrup before peeling the pears. Add the sugar, cinnamon stick, ground cloves and mace to the vinegar in a large saucepan. Bring slowly to the boil, stirring until the sugar is dissolved. Peel, core and quarter the pears (halving the quarters if they are large) and add to the syrup as you prepare them. Simmer gently until tender, divide the pears between two small or three larger jars, and pour the syrup over them. It should be sufficient to cover the fruit. Seal at once.

Spiced grape butter

Imperial/metric
2 lb./1 kg. black grapes
1 pint/6 dl. water
2 tablespoons grated
  orange zest
1½ lb./700 g. sugar
1 teaspoon ground
  cinnamon
½ teaspoon ground cloves

American
2 lb. Concord grapes
2½ cups water
2 tablespoons grated
  orange rind
3 cups sugar
1 teaspoon ground
  cinnamon
½ teaspoon ground cloves

Cook the grapes in the water until soft. Sieve to remove the seeds and skins. Add the orange zest, sugar and spices to the grape pulp. Cook over low heat until thick. Pour into hot clean jars. Seal. Makes about 2 lb./1 kg.

Pickled cherries

Imperial/metric
¾ pint/4 dl. water
¼ pint/1½ dl. white
  vinegar
2 oz./50 g. sugar
1 cinnamon stick
½ teaspoon whole allspice
½ teaspoon whole cloves
½ teaspoon salt
1½ lb./¾ kg. fresh red
  cherries

American
2 cups water
½ cup white vinegar
¼ cup granulated sugar
1 cinnamon stick
½ teaspoon whole allspice
½ teaspoon whole cloves
½ teaspoon salt
1½ lb. cherries

Combine the water, vinegar, sugar, spices and salt in a saucepan. Bring to the boil and simmer for 5 minutes. Wash the cherries, leaving the stems on. Pack the cherries into clean jars. Pour the hot liquid over the cherries, leaving ½ inch/1 cm. headspace. Seal tightly. Place the sealed jars in a boiling bath and boil for 5 minutes. Remove and test seal. Let stand for 2 weeks before using. Drain before serving. Serve with ham or cold meats. Makes about 2 lb./1 kg.

Hot pepper jelly

Imperial/Metric
2 lb./1 kg. red or green
  peppers
2 chilli peppers
3 lb./1½ kg. sugar
½ pint/3 dl. vinegar
¼ pint/1½ dl. water
6 oz./175 ml. commercial
  pectin

American
2 lb. red or green peppers
2 chili peppers
6 cups granulated sugar
1¼ cups vinegar
½ cup water
1 6 oz. bottle fruit pectin

Mince the peppers separately and drain the pulp well, reserving the juice. In a large saucepan, place ½ pint/3 dl. of the pepper juice and 2 fl. oz./50 ml. of the chilli pepper juice. Add the sugar, vinegar and water: bring to the boil and stir in the pectin. Boil vigorously for 1 minute. Remove from the heat, let stand, then remove the foam. Pour into hot clean jars. Seal.
Makes 1½ pints/scant 1 litre or 4 cups.

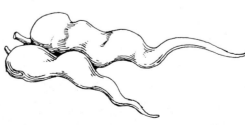

Spiced gooseberry relish

Imperial/metric
2 lb./1 kg.
  gooseberries
8 oz./225 g. white sugar
4 oz./125 g. soft brown
  sugar
$\frac{1}{4}$ pint/1$\frac{1}{2}$ dl. white vinegar
$\frac{1}{4}$ pint/1$\frac{1}{2}$ dl. water
5 whole cloves
1 stick cinnamon
$\frac{1}{2}$ teaspoon ground allspice

American
2 lb. gooseberries
2 cups light sugar
1 cup brown sugar
$\frac{1}{2}$ cup white vinegar
$\frac{1}{2}$ cup water
5 whole cloves
1 stick cinnamon
$\frac{1}{2}$ teaspoon allspice

Wash and remove the stems from the gooseberries. Combine all the ingredients in a large saucepan. Cook over low heat until thickened, about 45 minutes. Remove the cloves and cinnamon stick. Pour into hot clean jars. Seal.
Makes 1$\frac{1}{2}$ pints/scant 1 litre/4 cups.

Cinnamon peach butter

Imperial/Metric
4 lb./2 kg. peaches
scant $\frac{1}{2}$ pint/3 dl. water
3 lb./1$\frac{1}{4}$ kg. sugar
1 teaspoon ground
  cinnamon
$\frac{1}{2}$ teaspoon ground cloves

American
4 lb. peaches
1 cup water
3 lb. sugar
1 teaspoon ground
  cinnamon
½ teaspoon ground cloves

Halve and stone the peaches. Slice roughly and cook gently in the water until tender. Sieve or liquidise in a blender goblet. Add the sugar and spices. Bring slowly to the boil and cook over low heat, stirring occasionally, until thick; about the consistency of unwhipped cream. Pour into warm clean jars and seal. This relish, spread thinly on buttered bread, makes a delicious sandwich combined with sliced cold park, ham, or beef.

Strawberry and rhubarb freezer relish

Imperial/Metric
2 lb./1 kg. rhubarb
1 lb./450 g. sugar
1 lb./450 g. strawberries
1 4$\frac{1}{2}$ oz./127 g. packet
  strawberry jelly
$\frac{1}{2}$ teaspoon ground nutmeg

American
2 lb. rhubarb
2 cups granulated sugar
1 lb. strawberries
1$\frac{1}{2}$ 3 oz. packets strawberry
  flavored gelatin
$\frac{1}{2}$ teaspoon ground nutmeg

Cut the rhubarb into 1 inch/2.5 cm. pieces, and place in a large saucepan. Add sugar and nutmeg and let stand overnight. Add the strawberries and bring to the boil. Remove from heat and stir in the strawberry jelly. Let cool, then pour into polythene containers. Freeze. To serve, defrost at room temperature for 30 minutes. Store in the refrigerator after defrosting.

Come to a barbecue

For entertaining without a fuss, plan a barbecue party . . . Keep the menu simple and be prepared for large outdoor appetites. Recipes are to serve 12.

Light the fire at least 30 minutes before your guests arrive. To prepare the fire for a portable barbecue, line the base of the barbecue pan with foil and a layer of gravel. This makes cleaning up easier and provides ventilation for the fire. Pile the charcoal briquettes in the centre of the barbecue pan and set alight. Allow it to burn for 30 minutes or until the coals are covered with a grey ash. Arrange the coals over the base of the barbecue pan. Rub the grill rack with oil to prevent the food from sticking to it, and place it over the hot coals. Place the food on the grill so that pieces do not touch. Use long tongs to turn the food and keep a sprinkling can of water handy to douse flames from dripping fat. To keep the fire going, set extra charcoal briquettes around the edge of the barbecue pan to warm up before adding them to the fire. This will help to eliminate smoke from the fire.

Practically any of the meats you grill or fry in the kitchen can be cooked on the barbecue. Chops, steaks, sausages, frankfurters and beefburgers are favourites as they are quick-cooking and need little preparation.

Menu

Jumbo beefburgers with Chilli barbecue sauce
Cheesey frankfurters
Sweet and sour sausages
Mexicali salad
Crunchy crisp dip
Liver sausage whip
Potato crisps
Savoury biscuits
Honeyed fruit kebabs
Toasted coconut squares
Cartwheel bananas
Light ale or lager
Lemonade shandy

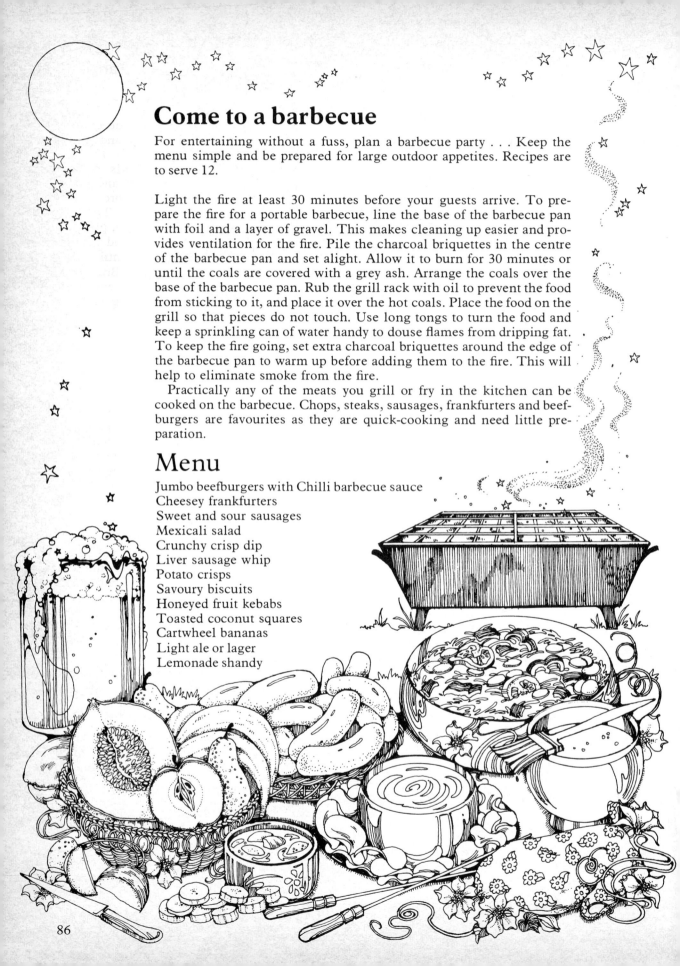

Jumbo beefburgers

Imperial/Metric
2 lb./1 kg. minced beef
1 large onion, finely
   chopped
2 teaspoons salt
$\frac{1}{4}$ teaspoon pepper
$\frac{1}{4}$ teaspoon dry mustard
3 tablespoons ketchup
2 eggs, beaten

American
2 lb. ground beef
1 large onion, finely
   chopped
2 teaspoons salt
$\frac{1}{4}$ teaspoon pepper
$\frac{1}{4}$ teaspoon dry mustard
3 tablespoons catsup
2 eggs, beaten

Mix the minced beef with the chopped onion, seasonings, ketchup and beaten eggs. Roll the mixture into 12 balls. Place the minced meat balls between squares of greaseproof paper and roll to $\frac{1}{2}$ inch/1 cm. thickness. Store in the refrigerator until required. Transport in insulated bag. To barbecue, place the beefburgers over hot coals and grill for 5 minutes on each side or until cooked through and nicely browned. Brush both sides of each beefburger frequently with Chilli barbecue sauce during cooking. Serve in buttered soft rolls.

Cheesey frankfurters

Imperial/Metric
12 frankfurters
6 oz./175 g. Cheddar
   cheese
12 rashers lean bacon
12 long rolls
French mustard

American
12 frankfurters
6 oz. Cheddar cheese
12 slices back bacon
12 long rolls
prepared mustard

Cut a lengthwise slit down each frankfurter. Divide the cheese into 12 narrow pieces. Fill the slit in each frankfurter with a piece of cheese. Wrap the bacon securely around the frankfurters. Place over hot coals and grill until the bacon is crisp. Serve in rolls spread with mustard.

Chilli barbecue sauce

Imperial/Metric
1 large onion, finely
   chopped
2 tablespoons vinegar
2 tablespoons
   Worcestershire sauce
1 teaspoon mild chilli
   powder
$\frac{1}{4}$ pint/1$\frac{1}{2}$ dl. water
$\frac{1}{4}$ pint/1$\frac{1}{2}$ dl. ketchup
3 tablespoons cooking oil

American
1 large onion, finely
   chopped
2 tablespoons vinegar
2 tablespoons
   Worcestershire sauce
1 teaspoon mild chili
   powder
generous $\frac{1}{2}$ cup water
generous $\frac{1}{2}$ cup catsup
3 tablespoons cooking oil

Place all the ingredients in a small saucepan. Cover and simmer for 15 minutes. Cool and store in a covered container in the refrigerator. Use as required. Makes $\frac{1}{2}$ pint/3 dl. sauce.

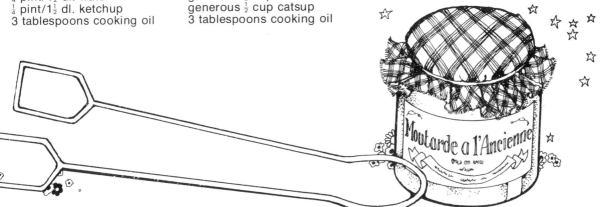

Moutarde a l'Ancienne

Sweet and sour sausages

Imperial/Metric
6 oz./175 g. sugar
¼ pint/1½ dl. vinegar
3 fl. oz./75 ml. water
1 tablespoon chopped
   green pepper
1 tablespoon chopped
   pimiento
2 teaspoons cornflour
¼ teaspoon salt
1 teaspoon paprika pepper
12 beef or pork chipolatas

American
¾ cup sugar
generous ½ cup vinegar
generous ⅓ cup water
1 tablespoon chopped
   green pepper
1 tablespoon chopped
   pimiento
2 teaspoons cornstarch
¼ teaspoon salt
1 teaspoon paprika pepper
12 thin pork links

Combine the sugar, vinegar, water, chopped green pepper and pimiento in a small saucepan. Bring to the boil and simmer for 5 minutes. Moisten the cornflour and salt with a little cold water and slowly stir into the hot liquid. Cook, stirring constantly, until the sauce is thick. Cool, then add the paprika. Grill the sausages over hot coals, turning frequently and brushing with the sauce. Serve with toasted rolls and hand extra sauce separately.

 # Mexicali salad

Imperial/Metric
1 lb./450 g. carrots
1 lb./450 g. white cabbage
1 green pepper
1 bunch spring onions
1 bunch radishes
4 tomatoes
½ pint/3 dl. French
   dressing

American
1 lb. carrots
1 lb. cabbage
1 green pepper
1 bunch scallions
1 bunch radishes
4 tomatoes
1¼ cups Italian dressing

Shred the carrots and cabbage coarsely. Chop the green pepper and the onions. Slice the radishes and dice the tomatoes. Toss the prepared vegetables with the dressing. Refrigerate for 1 hour to blend the flavours.

 # Liver sausage whip

Imperial/Metric
4 oz./125 g. liver sausage
3 oz./87 g. cream cheese
2 tablespoons chopped
   parsley
4 fl. oz./100 ml. double
   cream
garlic salt and pepper

American
¼ lb. liverwurst
3 oz. package cream cheese
2 tablespoons chopped
   parsley
½ cup whipping cream
garlic salt and pepper

Mash the liver sausage until very smooth. Beat into the cream cheese. Stir in the chopped parsley. Whip the cream until thick and fold into the cheese mixture. Season to taste. Serve with potato crisps and small savoury biscuits.

Crunchy crisp dip

Imperial/Metric
3 oz./87 g. cream cheese
2 teaspoons ketchup
1 teaspoon made mustard
pinch ground ginger
2 oz./50 g. crumbled
  cooked bacon
5 tablespoons soured
  cream

American
3 oz. package cream cheese
2 teaspoons catsup
1 teaspoon prepared
  mustard
dash ground ginger
½ cup crumbled cooked
  bacon
generous ⅓ cup soured
  cream

Soften the cream cheese. Beat in the remaining ingredients until well blended. Refrigerate for 1 hour to blend flavours. Serve with potato crisps and small savoury biscuits.

Sweet afterthoughts: When the fire is getting low, serve barbecued desserts which require a low heat, or set a pan on the grid to heat up a ready-made sauce to pour over ice cream or a cream layered cake.

Melba sauce: This is a sauce which can be made with previously frozen raspberry purée. Heat ½ pint/3 dl./1¼ cups raspberry purée (sieved if liked to remove the seeds) in a saucepan. Blend 1 tablespoon cornflour with 1 tablespoon water and stir into the purée. Cook over a low heat, stirring all the time, until the sauce thickens. Add 2 oz./50 g./¼ cup castor sugar and the grated zest and juice of 1 lemon.

Honey sauce: Melt 3 oz/75 g./6 tablespoons butter in a saucepan and stir in 2 teaspoons cornflour. Gradually add 8 oz./225 g./1 cup clear honey and bring to the boil, stirring. Cook for 1-2 minutes. Add 1 teaspoon lemon juice.

Honeyed fruit kebabs

Imperial/Metric
4 fl. oz./125 ml. honey
3 tablespoons lemon juice
2 oz./50 g. butter
2 dessert apples, 2 pears,
1 small melon

American
½ cup honey
3 tablespoons lemon juice
¼ cup butter
2 eating apples, 2 pears,
1 small melon

First make the honey butter sauce. Combine the honey, lemon juice and butter in a saucepan and stir over heat until well blended. Dip wedges of unpeeled apples, fresh pears, and melon cubes in the honey butter sauce. Thread alternately on long metal skewers and grill over a low fire until the fruit is glazed and heated through. Brush occasionally with the sauce and turn often to avoid scorching.

Toasted coconut squares: Dip 2 inch/5 cm. squares of sponge cake into clear honey or sweetened condensed milk. Roll in desiccated coconut. Thread the cake pieces on long skewers and toast over the coals until the coconut turns golden.

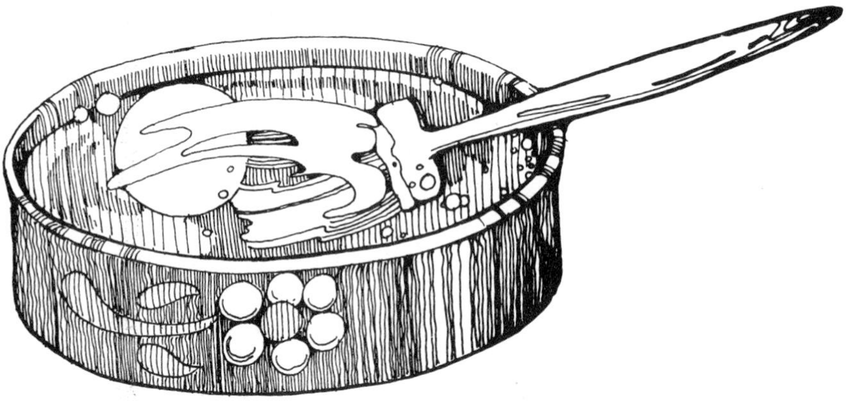

Cart-wheel bananas: Leave the peel on firm bananas. Cut in diagonal slices, about 1 inch/2.5 cm. thick. Dip the cut ends in lemon juice, then coat with a mixture of brown sugar and cinnamon. Thread on long skewers, alternating with thick, unpeeled orange slices. Grill until the banana skin turns brown. Even the skins can be eaten.

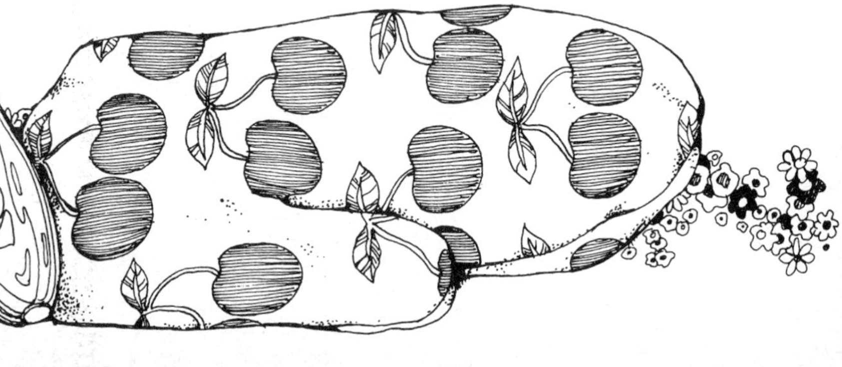

Storing wine leftovers

With the ever-increasing popularity of wine, the bottle with an inch or two remaining is less rare a sight in the kitchen. Do not waste it: small quantities of wine can be frozen and used to flavour and enhance many dishes. Do not mix red and white wines, but store them separately in polythene containers—a midget Tupperware tumbler is ideal for this purpose. Be sure to label the container white or red. Alternatively the wine may be frozen in an ice tray and the cubes packed in a polythene bag. Use red wine cubes for beef and game casseroles; white wine cubes will enliven a white sauce for fish and delicate poultry dishes. Simply add the frozen wine cube to the rest of the liquid in the recipe.

If you know you can use the leftover wine within the next 2-3 days, transfer to a small container to avoid contact with air inside the bottle and consequent oxidation, and keep it in the refrigerator. Use it up in casseroles, etc.

The flavour and texture of meat is improved if it is frozen in a marinade and wine leftovers can be utilised in a marinade. For kebabs or stews, cut the meat up into cubes and place in a polythene container. Cover with a marinade, seal, label and freeze. When the time comes to cook the meat, use the marinade in the recipe—either as part of the liquid if it is for braising, or use to brush the meat with while cooking if it is for grilling. Other ways of using leftover wine include adding it to dishes you are making to freeze; a bolognaise or tomato sauce to serve with pasta; soups, sauces and pâtés; ice creams and sorbets. All these dishes freeze successfully and will be improved with the addition of a little wine which might otherwise have been wasted.

INDEX